M000287528

ISBN
978-1-09834-806-9

Edited by J. Marc Replogle

Cover design and layout by Jeanne Sperry

**NOTE TO READER**

Thank you for reading Miracles and the Messenger.
May I suggest you consider reading this book slowly,
in a contemplative manner.
You may want to read one chapter at a time,
one day at a time.
There is much to consider.
May you be blessed.

# INTRODUCTION

In April of 2019, God gave me a very specific dream in which He showed me this book. In obedience, and with a lot of prayer, I have written what He has asked me to write. This book is my testimony. It contains some of the many miracles God has done for or through me or to which I have been witness. This book tells of His amazing, transformative power in my own life and also contains dreams, visions, and words He has given me to help lift and encourage His people. He loves us all so very deeply and wants us to know we all are seen, heard, and loved. He is mindful of us. The events in this book jump around in time, but I have written this book in the way He has instructed me. In reading this book, you will see God and know He exists, regardless of where you are in your life. Your faith will be strengthened, and you will be encouraged by the love God has for everyone. You will see God's presence and activity in these current times. Above all, I pray this book points to God and glorifies Him.

All scripture used is from the NIV unless stated otherwise.

**I will pour out my Spirit on all people.**
**Your sons and daughters will prophesy.**
**Your young men will see visions,**
**your old men will dream dreams.**

Joel 2:28 and Acts 2:17

Here's another way to put it:
You're here to be a light,
bringing out the God-colors in the world.
God is not a secret to be kept.
We're going public with this, as public as a city on a hill.
If I make you light-bearers, you don't think I am going to
hide you under a bucket, do you?
I'm putting you on a light stand.
Now that I've put you there on a hilltop,
on a light stand – shine!
Keep open house; be generous with your lives.
By opening up to others,
you'll prompt people to open up with God,
this generous Father in heaven.

Matthew 5:14-16  MSG

# CHAPTER 1

## WELCOME THE STRANGER

**No one can deliver out of my hand.**
**When I act, who can reverse it?**
Isaiah 43:13

**No one will snatch them out of my hand.**
John 10:28

In 2004, I was given a second chance at life after struggling with B-cell lymphoma and blood clots as well as the many side effects caused by chemotherapy and radiation. With the help of God and man, I was healed. In gratitude of my second chance, I wanted to glorify God with the gifts I had been given. I am an artist, having studied art in college; and for many years after I was healed, I had difficulty finding my way as an artist. I tried different mediums and means of selling art, but I did not know exactly what I should do.

In the fall of 2013, I decided to apply to a small, holiday craft show at a local church located about three miles from my home. I had never been a vendor at a craft show. It was completely new for me. I was nervous about talking to people and for them to see my work. As an artist, my work is personal and an extension of my heart. Thoughts were going through my head like, "What if no one likes it?" However, God had healed me, and I really wanted to honor Him and share all He had done on my behalf. My love of God outweighed my fear. That small craft show was a way for me to begin. I thought, "What do I have to lose?"

I set up a table with some original artwork and art prints in my assigned space the day before the craft show. On the morning of the show, while driving to the church, I said a prayer. I simply asked God to use me how He wanted on that day and that He be glorified.

My booth was in the main entryway of the church and was very visible to all who walked in the front door. As I was sitting behind my table in my booth, waiting for customers to arrive, I looked out the front door and saw a man walking up the steps of the church. Something did not seem right about him. He was dressed all in black, from head to toe, including a long black leather coat and gloves. As I was staring at him, he stumbled on the steps leading up to the church. He began talking to himself and looked angry. Something was very wrong with this man, but I heard God say loudly, "Welcome the stranger."

When the man entered the church, I left my seat from behind the table where I was sitting in my booth. I went to meet him and welcome him as God told me to do, even though he looked troubled and intimidating. I smiled at him and said, "Hi, welcome. It looked like you stumbled out there. Are you okay?"

He replied, "If only stumbling were the worst of my problems. I need someone to pray for me." Just then, tears started to run down his face as he began to sob.

I said, "I will pray for you." I asked his name, and I grabbed his hands to not only pray with him, but also because I was concerned he may have a weapon. I began to pray how God was leading me. I spoke words of love, compassion, and mercy over him. I do not know or remember all that I spoke. I just tried to let God speak through me to this troubled, hurting man. As I prayed, I heard God say, "Don't commit the crime that is in your heart." I spoke those words out loud, and the man began to cry harder. His knees buckled as he sank to the ground. I kept hold of his hands and sank down to the floor with him. I could see how distressed he was after speaking these words. I then asked him as kindly as I possibly could, "Why are you crying? What is the problem?"

He replied, "I just got out of prison. I came home to find out my wife is having an affair with my best friend. I was on my way to kill them or to kill myself, because I just can't live in this kind of pain anymore." My heart broke for this man. I stayed on the ground with him and continued to pray with him and hold his hands.

Meanwhile, people were gathering around us, because I was on the floor in the entryway of the church with this man who was sobbing. I began to feel I was out of my league and did not know what to do next. I said a silent prayer and asked God for help. At that moment, a man walked up to us and introduced himself as the music minister of the church. He helped us off the ground and began to lead us to a quiet room in an area away from the crowd that was forming around us. Later, I learned the music minister had actually been involved in prison ministry, an experience I am sure was helpful in this situation. He was not normally at the church on Saturday, but said he had to stop by for something he needed for Sunday's service.

The music minister gave the man a cup of coffee and began to speak gently to him and ask how he could help the man. I saw the man for whom I was praying was in good hands. I did not feel I was needed any further.

In relief, I left and went back to my booth and sat down in a daze. I said to the Lord, "What was that? Wow!" I was just stunned and in awe. Then God turned my attention to one of my art prints. This particular print was one of the first pieces I made after my battle with lymphoma. The piece depicted The Lord triumphing over evil. God impressed upon me to give the print to the man.

In obedience, I once again got up from the table at my booth, picked up the print, and walked back to the room where the music minister and the man were still together. I said, "Excuse me sir, God wanted me to give this to you. I created it after a very difficult time in my life. It is about God triumphing over evil; and I want you to have it." Then I handed it to him.

He looked at the art print and looked at me. He looked at the art print again and looked at me again. Then he said, "You had cancer."

I said, "Yes sir, I did."

"It was in your chest."

"Yes sir, it was."

Then he said, "Now I know why the Lord sent me to you. You see, when I was young, my mother had breast cancer. God did a healing miracle in her. I have forgotten the Lord."

I was stunned and in complete awe. I thanked him and, once again, went back to sit behind the table in my booth.

While sitting in my booth and in awe of God, I simply tried to process all that had just happened. After a little while, one of the volunteers who was working at the craft show came to me and said, "I wanted to let you know that we called the police. We had to, because he threatened to kill himself and others. When the police arrived and were putting him in the police car, he told me to tell you he had a message for you." I asked her, "What is the message?" The volunteer said, "He told me to tell you that, because you helped him, God told him to tell you that you would be protected by God all the days of your life." Once again, I was in complete awe of the Lord and all that he had done.

Several weeks later, while shopping in Target, I ran into the woman who was in charge of the craft show. We spoke of the wonders the Lord had done on that day. She said her Sunday school class and church were continuing to pray for the man. She then told me my booth was not supposed to be in the spot where they had assigned me that day. Prior to the day the vendors set up for the show, they marked off booth spaces and assigned numbers to the spaces. Each vendor was assigned a booth number and space where they were to set up. When the volunteers finished marking off spaces that evening, they realized a particular vendor needed an electrical outlet, but did not have one at their assigned space. They then noticed mine had an outlet, but I did not need electricity. The last thing they did that day before leaving the church was to switch us. They moved my assigned spot to the entryway of the church so the other vendor could have electricity and, as orchestrated by God, so I could welcome the stranger.

I am always in awe of how detailed the Lord is and to what great lengths He will go to reach and redeem us. He loves and desires us so. Even when we fail, wander away, and cannot keep our promises, He is true to His character and always keeps His word. Indeed, no one will be snatched from His hand.

# CHAPTER 2

## LYMPHOMA

**I am the Lord who heals you.**

Exodus 15:26

**I can do all things through Christ who strengthens me.**

Philippians 4:13 NKJV

In the spring of 2003, I was outside doing yard work with my husband. My children were running around and playing. It was a beautiful, bright spring day. All of the azaleas and dogwoods were blooming. The trees were the beautiful chartreuse I long to see each spring. I love seeing that shade of green next to the clear, bright, blue sky. I was enjoying a time of peace in my life. As I was working, I began to think of my grandmothers and great grandmother who had all passed away. They all had left a great impression, not only on me, but on others with their love of the Lord and their faith in Him. At that moment, though, I did not actually feel like I really knew the Lord. Did I even love Him? I recall saying a prayer, "Jesus, I really don't know you. Who are you? I want to know you."

A few months later, while on vacation, I slipped on some water and fell down a cement stairwell. I hurt my back and neck and could hardly move. After a few months, as fall approached, I was not improving. I still had significant pain, and I developed a cough that would not go away. My cough kept getting worse, and I began to have trouble breathing. Meanwhile, a small lump had formed under my arm. I went to see a doctor who pre-scribed antibiotics and gave me an inhaler, which seemed to not work at all. My condition actually worsened. Early in the week of Thanksgiving, 2003, I still was not improving, and my breathing was becoming more labored. Before the holiday, when it may have been more difficult to see a doctor, I called my doctor's office; and they told me to give the antibiotics another day or two to work, and if I were not feeling any better by the Friday af-ter Thanksgiving, to come back in, and they would take another look at me. I did not make it to that Friday.

On Thanksgiving morning, my precious husband told me to sleep in so I could feel better. He said he would get all the food preparations started and, if I felt better, to come down later and help with our Thanksgiving meal.

Unfortunately, I was having trouble sleeping, because I was still having difficulty breathing. I had been trying everything to sleep, changing positions and even propping up on pillows. I felt so tired and awful, but I thought I would take a shower, which sometimes makes me feel better, and go downstairs and try to help my husband. During my shower, I noticed how badly my left arm hurt and that I could hardly lift it.

When I got out of the shower, I looked in the mirror; and to my horror, I saw my neck was swollen, and all the veins in my neck were distended. Moreover, my face was discolored, swollen, and pale, almost white. I dried off, put on some clothes, and called to my husband. He immediately came upstairs and was followed by my children. Even though it was Thanksgiving morning, we agreed I needed to call my doctor.

We called my doctor, and he told me to go immediately to the emergency room, right away. My husband, who had heated the oven just before putting in the turkey, turned off the oven, put all the food back in the refrigerator, packed me and our children in the car, and drove to the Kennestone Hospital Emergency Room.

Thankfully, the Emergency Room was not crowded on Thanksgiving morning, and I was quickly seen by a doctor. They did a chest X-Ray; and I could tell by the look on the nurse's face something was terribly wrong. I was immediately admitted to the hospital, and sadly, I was not going home for Thanksgiving.

While waiting to be transferred to a hospital room, my husband took our two children to our neighbor's house, about twenty minutes away, and thankfully, they were home. My husband could hardly talk to our neighbors. He was scared, not knowing what was happening, but they were happy to help. They loved on our children and shared Thanksgiving dinner with them.

As I was still waiting in the Emergency Room for my husband to return, I was crying and very scared. Two kind and loving nurses each got on one side of me, and each held one of my hands. They spoke kindly to me and stayed with me. I was so grateful for their presence. Throughout my illness, whenever I was hospitalized, which was often, they would make the effort to find me and check on me, even though they were working in another area of the hospital.

When my husband returned, a doctor told us the X-Ray showed a mass in my chest, but did not commit to anything specific. With no diagnosis yet, and two young children at a neighbor's house for eight to ten hours, my husband went home late that night to get our children and stay with them. We had them stay with other friends on Friday, and my husband returned to the hospital early the next morning.

That Friday, after finally getting into a room, while my husband was with me, we were told that they were looking for cancer. I cried, and my husband and I held each other. The first thought that went through my mind was all the time I had wasted being angry, bitter, and unforgiving, when I could have been loving people around me.

The second thought gripped me with an even greater fear. I thought, "I am going to die and go before God and have to give an accounting for my life. I have done absolutely nothing with the gifts He has given me. I have done nothing for Him." I prayed and begged God to save me.

At that moment, my husband made a conscious decision that he would do whatever was needed to help me, no matter what. He went into what we now call *automatic pilot* mode.

A biopsy was scheduled for and performed Sunday morning. When I came out of surgery, and while waking up from the anesthesia, I could see doctors and nurses rushing around me. There were two nurses standing next to me, one on each side; but I also saw someone else standing there too. I saw my father, who had passed away when I was fourteen years old. I looked at him and he at me. Then he silently turned to leave. I saw him walk off and then disappear at the end of the hallway. I called to him. I told the nurses who were beside me, "There is my dad! He is right there! Bring him back to me! He is right over there." I tried to raise my hand to point where he was, but it was too difficult. Both of the nurses looked, but neither saw him.

Even though I was not fully awake from the anesthesia, I was packed into an ambulance. My husband rode with us. I was taken across the street to the radiation center. The center was closed on Sunday; but a nurse and the radiation doctor, who was in his Sunday best, having been called out of church to help, opened the center to begin immediate treatment on me.

After my first radiation treatment, I was packed back into the ambulance and taken back to the hospital, where I was placed in ICU.

While in ICU, an oncologist I did not know, but for whom I was and am very grateful, came in and told me and my husband I had B-cell lymphoma. My condition was very serious, yet treatable. I had a large tumor, 9.8 x 6.4 centimeters in the center of my chest that was between my lungs and covering my heart and trachea. The tumor was the size of a baseball. It was one millimeter from my heart, which was why they began radiation treatments immediately. They were trying to keep the rapidly growing lymphoma tumors from spreading and moving to Stage 4, which could have been any minute, any hour, any day. I also had other satellite tumors in my neck and chest that were strangling me, making it difficult to breathe. My doctor then told me, "I know your family history. You must look forward and be positive. If you are not, it could mean your life." Although they had different types of lymphoma, both my father and grandfather had lymphoma, and they died young. I was about the same age as my dad when he was diagnosed with lymphoma. At that moment, I made a conscious choice. I decided I would look for God every day. I decided this generational illness would go no further than me.

I spent the next three days in ICU. I remember a nurse coming in and rousing me every now and then and telling me to breathe. She said I was taking only one breath per minute. I also remember being packed up every day and being taken by ambulance to the radiation center for treatment to not only stop the spread, but also to allow me to breathe. I literally was being strangled by the tumors.

I remember the painful bone marrow test where they stuck a long needle into my femur through my hip.

I remember the two men who were a part of my husband's Bible study coming into my room. They anointed me with oil and prayed for healing for me. "Is anyone among you sick? Let them call the elders of the church to pray over them and anoint them with oil in the name of the Lord. And the prayer offered in faith will make the sick person well: The Lord will raise them up." James 5:14,15, NIV.

I remember being told many people had been praying for me in the waiting room outside ICU, every day I was there.

After three days, I was stable enough to be moved out of ICU and onto the oncology ward where they began chemotherapy. I was given CHOPS Rituxan, one of the most powerful chemotherapies at that time. They had to give it to me at an extremely slow drip, because I began to feel unusual symptoms in my heart. I eventually came home eight days later. Thanksgiving had come and gone, and it was well into December.

# CHAPTER 3

## MIRACLES

*He will call on me, and I will answer him;*
*I will be with him in trouble,*
*I will deliver him and honor him.*
*With long life I will satisfy him*
*and show him my salvation.*

Psalm 91:14 - 16

After my first chemotherapy treatment, when I was finally allowed to go home from the hospital, I developed a "problem." I had been home less than ten days, since my initial eight-day stay that began Thanksgiving morning, and was lying in bed when I started to feel numbness and tingling in my legs and arms. I soon became unresponsive. I could hear my family; and when I was able to crack open my eyes, I could see them, but it was extremely difficult to move and respond. It was evening, and my husband called the oncology doctor on call who advised us to go back to the Emergency Room at Kennestone Hospital, immediately. She said I may be having a stroke as a result of the chemotherapy. My husband picked me up and carried me to the car, as I could not even walk, and drove me to the hospital.

When we arrived, I was taken back to a room right away. Once again, I could hear everything going on around me, but I could neither feel my body nor respond to anyone. I felt completely numb. Once I was safely back in a room and my husband had spoken to the nurse about all that was going on, he then left to go move our car out of the emergency lane and park it, as he had simply pulled up to the Emergency Room, left the car, and carried me inside.

While he was gone, and I was lying in the room waiting to be seen by a doctor, a man was wheeled into the room with me. He had just been hit by a car. He was severely injured and was screaming and crying in pain. The nurses were cutting off his clothes in order to treat him and prep him for emergency surgery.

As I was lying there and listening, I heard the nurses ask him a series of questions. They asked, "Do you have family we can call?"

The man responded, "I just moved here a couple of days ago. I ain't got no family."

"Do you have a neighbor we can call?"

"I ain't got no place to live."

"Do you have an employer we can call?"

"I ain't got no job. I just moved here."

"Do you have a church or pastor we can call?"

"I ain't got no church or no pastor. I am all alone. I ain't got nobody."

He just lay there on the hospital bed, surrounded by nurses who had rushed to treat him while he cried and screamed. My heart broke for him.

I began to pray for him to be healed and to find a church home. I prayed he would know the love and mercy of God. I prayed he would know Christ. After I prayed for the man, I began to think how blessed I was to have a loving family and church who were all helping both me and my husband. They were taking care of our children and cooking meals while I was in the hospital and while my husband worked and otherwise stayed by my side. They truly were a gift. Shortly thereafter, they wheeled the man away for surgery.

I continued to think how blessed I was and how great, good, and powerful God is. I was grateful for the opportunity to silently pray for the injured man while in my hospital bed. I began to think of God's promises and character while lying there, waiting for my husband to return. I then remembered one of my favorite Bible passages, Psalm 91. Interestingly, this Psalm was given to my husband in 1997, as a verse to read regularly and pray on, by the same man who had anointed me with oil in ICU just two weeks prior.

### Psalm 91 reads:

Whoever dwells in the shelter of the Most High
will rest in the shadow of the Almighty.
I will say of the Lord, "He is my refuge and my fortress,
my God, in whom I trust."
Surely he will save you
from the fowler's snare
and from the deadly pestilence.
He will cover you with his feathers,
and under his wings you will find refuge;
his faithfulness will be your shield and rampart.
You will not fear the terror of night,
nor the arrow that flies by day,
nor the pestilence that stalks in the darkness,
nor the plague that destroys at midday.
A thousand may fall at your side,
ten thousand at your right hand,
but it will not come near you.
You will only observe with your eyes
and see the punishment of the wicked.
If you say, "The Lord is my refuge,"
and you make the Most High your dwelling,
no harm will overtake you,
no disaster will come near your tent.
For he will command his angels concerning you
to guard you in all your ways;
they will lift you up in their hands,
so that you will not strike your foot against a stone.
You will tread on the lion and the cobra;
you will trample the great lion and the serpent.
"Because he loves me," says the Lord, "I will rescue him;
I will protect him, for he acknowledges my name.
He will call on me, and I will answer him;
I will be with him in trouble,
I will deliver him and honor him.
With long life I will satisfy him
and show him my salvation."

I cried out to God in a silent, deep prayer from my inner being and said, "I love You! This is Your promise! Your promise is to protect me and that no disaster will come near me! I am calling You on Your promises God! Help me!"

Immediately after my plea, I began to regain the feeling in my body and was able to move. When my husband returned a few minutes later, I was sitting up in the hospital bed. I had all of my feeling back, and I was able to speak again. I was discharged without a medical explanation and went home. Praise be to the God of miracles!

About a week later, I found myself back in the hospital, having developed a fever of 103° F. While in the hospital, over a period of several days, I started having severe pain in my neck, armpit, and chest. My doctor ordered a CT scan of my chest and neck and a sonogram for under my arm. The tests revealed three blood clots. One clot was in my left armpit, one in my left lung, and one in the left side of my jugular vein. All of these blood clots, while related, were in addition to the lymphoma tumors.

I was treated with blood thinners, and over time, the blood thinners dissolved the clots under my armpit and in my chest. Unfortunately, however, the clot in my jugular vein remained. After six months, if a clot has not dissolved with the help of blood thinners, and this one did not dissolve in six months, it becomes part of your body and is permanent. The treatment is to stay on blood thinners for the rest of your life.

I completed four to five months of chemotherapy and then about two months of radiation. I was pronounced "free and clear" of the lymphoma in May of 2004, thanks to the help of my doctors and my God, and to my family and friends who helped me stay positive and keep going to endure and overcome.

However, about a year and a half after my chemotherapy and radiation treatments were completed, I started to develop a sensitivity, rather an allergy, to the blood thinners I was taking. The site where the blood clot was located in my neck started to swell. The swelling went down my neck to the top of my chest and into my arm. The left side of my face drooped. I had difficulty breathing. At the time, in 2005, there were only a couple of thinners on the market. My doctor had rotated me through the thinners I could take, and when I developed a sensitivity to the last thinner, my options were out. Because of the location of the clot, in my jugular vein, they could not remove it with surgery. At my appointment, my doctor, the oncologist who was with me from the beginning, told me I was out of options for blood thinners and that there was nothing else he could do to help. As a final effort, though, he said he was would have a conference call with other doctors across the United States to see if there was anything that could be done to help me. He said it was extremely rare to be so sensitive to blood thinners. I was instructed to follow up with him on Friday, for another appointment to discuss his findings, if any. He basically told me to get my affairs in order.

When I went home, I sat at the kitchen table and tried to draw for a moment and look at the birds on my feeder outside the window. I was in complete shock at my doctor's news. When the shock began to wear off, and the news that there were no options for me, that I would die from the blood clot in my neck, reality began to settle in. I then moved to the couch, and I just sat there and began to sob. I had been through so much. I had been in ICU. I almost died at least twice. I had endured chemotherapy and radiation therapy. I had been in the hospital for various, related problems numerous times during my treatments, usually four to eight days at a time. I had suffered debilitating bone pain from a medication I was given to help my immune system. The pain was so severe I had to be hospitalized on several occasions. I was given 50 milligrams of Demerol every two to four hours around the clock for pain control, but the Demerol did not even begin to ease my suffering. I also had numerous medical procedures, including a hysterectomy, among other things. I had suffered much, and I was just tired. I had tried to be positive the whole time, but being positive all of a sudden became mentally exhausting.

As I sobbed, I began to pray to God, a new prayer. I said, "God, I am tired. I can't be positive anymore. I just can't do this anymore. Please do it for me."

I immediately heard this "pop" in my neck, and I felt different. The blood clot was gone.

I continued to take my blood thinners until I saw my doctor two days later. At my appointment, I told him what had happened. He said, "Let me get this straight, you prayed the blood clot away." I said, "Yes, I did." My doctor immediately did a sonogram on my neck, and there was no blood clot! He then made an appointment for me to have a CT scan to be sure the clot was gone or had not moved to another area in my body before they took me off the blood thinners. The CT results showed no blood clot!

There was no medical explanation. This time I was healed by God. The blood clot was gone! I have been off blood thinners since then. Praise be to the God of miracles!

# CHAPTER 4

## THE BODY OF CHRIST

*There are different kinds of gifts, but the same Spirit.*
*There are different kinds of service, but the same Lord.*
*There are different kinds of working,*
*but the same God works all of them in all men.*

1 Corinthians 12:4-6

During my treatments, I resolved to look for God every day to help stay positive and look forward. I wanted His Presence to be greater than my circumstances. Looking for God daily became almost like a delightful game for me. I would wait expectantly each day to see how He would present Himself. I was never disappointed when it came to the faithfulness of God showing Himself to me.

I often looked out my window, whether I was in the hospital, which was a lot, or at home, to witness God's creation. I loved the light of the moon and the nimbus surrounding it. The linear shapes of the barren trees in winter, lighted by the moon on the nights when I could not sleep, were beautiful. I loved the twinkling of the stars in the clear winter sky. I expectantly waited for the coming of dawn on difficult and painful nights. I would watch the darkness slowly change to light in my room, wherever I was, and my mood would lift and become hopeful. As spring approached in 2004, while I was taking chemotherapy treatments, I delighted in watching the barren trees begin to bud bright green and the flowers that would unfurl in various shades of purples, pinks, and creams. I thoroughly enjoyed watching all of the brightly colored birds at my feeder, which was a favorite pastime for me.

God's creation is beautiful and majestic to behold. Likewise, the Body of Christ in action is a powerful and beautiful force to witness and behold. It is like a great swell in the sea, gathering and becoming a giant wave—a wave of love. Not only would I see God through His creation, but He showed up daily through His Body as faithfully as the sun rose and set each and every day. His Spirit was poured out on me through His believers. I saw Jesus shine brightly in so many ways.

I saw Him in the two nurses who were there in the Emergency Room on that Thanksgiving Day. They held my hand and came to visit me every time I entered the hospital.

I saw Jesus in my friends who sat beside me while I lay in my hospital bed.

I saw Him in the anesthesiologist who prayed with me and my husband before my biopsy.

I saw Jesus in the radiation doctor who was on call and opened up the radiation center on a Sunday morning, breaking away early from his church just to treat me so the cancer would not spread to my heart.

I saw Jesus in my doctor and his staff, as they tirelessly treated, helped, and encouraged me.

I saw Him in a nurse who hugged me and held my hand as I cried when my hair began to fall out in handfuls and clumps. As it turned out, she was a neighbor of mine who just happened to be there on that day and at that moment.

I saw Jesus in another nurse who handed me a card, with her phone number and the phone number of her church, when I first received my diagnosis. She told me to call without hesitation if I needed someone to drive me to treatments, meals, or help with my children, or even if I just needed someone to talk with. She assured me her church had a team of people to help if needed.

I saw Jesus in our friend and fellow church member who was the first person to come to the hospital and pray with us.

I saw Jesus in my hairdresser who came to the hospital to cut my hair nice and short to ease the pain of seeing it all fall out.

I saw Jesus in the cleaning lady at the hospital who said in all sincerity, and in broken English, "I pray for you. You don't give up."

I saw Jesus in my loving husband who took his marriage vows seriously. At times, he literally carried me when I could not walk. He would hold my hand and tell me I was still his pretty wife, even though I had no hair, no eyebrows, and no eyelashes, and I was skin and bones. He was always present and always encouraging. He was my voice and advocate. Not only did my husband take his marriage vows seriously, but he honored a commitment we both made when I was unable to keep that commitment. We had committed to take our children to church every Sunday, and he kept that commitment throughout my treatments and beyond.

I saw the Lord in my daughter, who at the time was nine years old. She colored cards for me that said, "Get well mommy. I love you. I can help with anything." She helped our various family members who came from out of town to help our family when neither I nor my husband were home. She did so much to help, especially in caring for her little brother. Her strength and faith were unshakable. They still are.

I saw Jesus in my son, who was only five at the time. I often had to sit on the stairs to go up them on my bottom. I had very little strength. He would sit by me and go up each step with me slowly, one at a time. He would make sure I made it to bed, his little hand holding mine, guiding me along slowly. Once we arrived at my bed, he would pull back the covers and tuck me in, then pull up the covers and kiss my cheek. He handed me my Bible and told me, "If you want to pray now, you can. God is all around you now, and He will hear you."

I saw Jesus in all of my family members who came from other states and traveled long distances to help and to care for my children. He was in my brother who was at the hospital after I was first diagnosed. I woke up, and he was there at my side. Then, he went to my home and lovingly cared for my children. I saw Jesus in my sister who came many times to help. My sister even brought me a bunch of clothes so I could "shop" at home and to help me feel like I looked nice. She drew cartoons for me to help me laugh. I saw Jesus in my cousin who left her young family a few days to come and take care of mine. He was in my aunts who held my children and prayed with them at dinnertime and before bed. I found Him in my uncles who left their businesses they ran to come and care for me and my children. They would sit by my bed and minister to me and my husband. The Lord was in the forgiveness that was found when strained relationships were mended.

I saw Jesus in my husband's parents, as well as in his sister and her husband, when they each visited from out of state and took care of our children and home.

I saw Him in my neighbors who welcomed and cared for my children and gave them Thanksgiving dinner on the day I first entered the hospital. He was also in the neighborhood women who prepared and delivered a Thanksgiving meal, for the one we missed, when I came home in December. He was in the Christmas carols my neighbors sang outside my door. I saw Him in my neighbors who cared for my children in the middle of the night when my husband had to take me to the Emergency Room. They also sat by my bed during the day when I was home so my husband could work.

I saw Jesus at the church preschool where teachers loved, hugged, and comforted my son when I was absent. I saw Jesus in all of my son's classmate's mothers who cared for my son after school, whenever asked, without hesitation.

I saw the Lord in our music minister when he invited me to sit in the tech booth, which was in the balcony of our church, where no one could see me, but where I could watch my daughter in a church play. He did not want me to miss seeing my daughter.

I saw Jesus in a friend who came to my hospital room and helped me laugh that deep, true laugh only a close friend can bring forth. That kind of laughter was a welcomed and healing relief.

I saw the Lord in another friend who one day helped me out of my bed, sat me in a chair, and then like a disciple of Christ, washed my feet. She helped me back into bed, only then to set about cleaning my home, doing laundry, and caring for my children when they came home from school.

I saw Jesus in a mailbox full of cards from adults. Some of them I knew well and some I did not. All of them were praying for me and offering words of encouragement. He was also in the brightly colored cards colored in crayon and marker by children in a church I did not even know. They were all praying for me. They all brought a smile to my face and touched my heart. I treasured those handmade cards.

I saw His hand at work in a list of Catholic churches handed to me by a friend. She and her husband had spent days calling all of the Catholic churches in the area and asking that I be placed on their prayer list.

I saw Jesus in every pair of earrings and every necklace that bore the symbol of the cross. He was in every WWJD band and lanyard I saw in the hospital. I purposely looked for the cross on each person I encountered. It gave me hope and encouragement.

His love was in the countless meals brought to our home and in every call made to our home to check on me. Many people asked if I was okay, what could be done to help, and how could they pray for me. Their concern and love touched my heart.

My precious Lord and Savior was waiting in the doorway full of flowers at my home when I was told I could stop treatments and that the cancer was gone. The flowers had been placed there by numerous friends and neighbors.

Jesus was in the overwhelming feeling of love I had, almost like a big hug, when I was finally able to walk back into church, thank Him, be with His body, and worship Him again alongside other believers. I did not see, but I felt, all of the spoken and silent prayers lifted on my behalf by His Body in His Name. He heard them, and indeed, He answered.

He is in the scripture I held and hold onto every day.

This is but a small fraction of the ways I witnessed and experienced Jesus and the tremendous force and power of the Body of Christ in action. Seeing His Body at work for me, to help me, was one of the ways I personally entered a closer relationship with Jesus Christ. Seeing Him in others, and watching others live out their faith, was and is very powerful.

When we take Jesus into our hearts, He gives us His Holy Spirit to come and live within us. It is His Holy Spirit that comforts, guides, equips, and directs us. Jesus is present with us, as individuals as well as through His Body and in His Body of believers, which is magnificent indeed.

# CHAPTER 5

## A GLIMPSE OF HEAVEN

**I will go on to visions and revelations from the Lord.
I know a man in Christ who fourteen years ago was caught up
to the third heaven. Whether it was in the body or out of the
body I do not know — God knows.**

2 Corinthians 12:2

I want to preface this chapter by saying that until now, I have only shared this with my husband, my two children, and a very small handful of people whom I trust deeply. It has been a wonderment to me. I do not fully understand, and frankly, it has been a lot to process over the years. I have simply been seeking God all these years, what He wants of my life, how I can serve Him, and how do I share the gifts He has given me to encourage and strengthen His people.

I was lying in bed one night in 2006. It was less than a year after God had miraculously healed me of the blood clot in my jugular vein. I could not sleep. I was staring at the ceiling, when all of a sudden, a bright light appeared. I could hear the sound of angels singing. It was beautiful yet indescribable. I was captivated and in awe. As I listened to the angels singing, I felt myself being lifted and pulled up. I rose higher and higher. As I rose, I could see a wall comprised of white stones. I could see neither where the wall began nor where it ended. I could see neither how wide the wall was nor how tall it was. There were just white stones as far as I could see in all directions.

As I soared up the wall, I slowed as I came to an opening. In the opening, I could see angels. The angels were gathering the white stones in piles to help build the wall. After seeing this, I continued to soar upward.

Further up the wall, I began to slow once again. I saw the head of a lion. The lion was white stone and was also part of the wall. The lion was roaring. I suddenly exclaimed, "The Lion of Judah!" After this exclamation, I soared higher and higher and at an even greater speed. I just kept passing more and more stones in this great wall. I started to become frightened at the speed and height. Then, I was laid gently back onto my bed. I felt the gentleness, peace, and Presence of God.

I do not fully understand what all of that meant. I have been praying and searching for many years. While a mystery that may not be revealed until I pass from this earth into heaven, I keep trying to serve God as best I can, however He leads me. What I do know is what God's Word says in the scriptures below.

**Ephesians 2:19-22 says (but see all of Ephesians 2):**

Consequently, you are no longer foreigners and strangers,
but fellow citizens with God's people and also
members of his household, built on the foundation of the
apostles and prophets, with Christ Jesus himself as the chief
cornerstone. In him the whole building is joined together and
rises to become a holy temple in the Lord. And in him you too
are being built together to become a dwelling
in which God lives by his Spirit.

**1 Peter 2:4-6 reads:**

As you come to him, the living Stone—rejected by humans,
but chosen by God and precious to him—you also,
like living stones, are being built into a spiritual house
to be a holy priesthood, offering spiritual sacrifices
acceptable to God through Jesus Christ.
For in Scripture, it says:

"See, I lay a stone in Zion,
a chosen and precious cornerstone,
and the one who trusts in him
will never be put to shame."

**Revelation 2:17 says:**

I will also give that person a white stone with a new name
written on it, known only to the one who receives it.

# CHAPTER 6

## DARK NIGHT OF THE SOUL

*...for a little while you may have had to suffer grief*
*in all kinds of trials. These have come so that the proven*
*genuineness of your faith – of greater worth than gold,*
*which perishes even though refined by fire – may result in*
*praise, glory, and honor when Jesus Christ is revealed.*

1 Peter 1:7

**Take captive every thought to make it obedient to Christ.**

2 Corinthians 10:5

I walked, crawled, and cried through one of the most difficult but fruitful times in my life. It was much worse than cancer and lasted longer too, years longer. But now, however, I can truly look back at this experience with gratitude. When God plants a seed, the enemy, that is, Satan, does his best to rob and kill the seed. He is a thief and liar.

Dark night of the soul is a strong feeling of separation from God. In his book "Angels," Billy Graham spoke of his own dark night. He said,

> Once when I was going through a dark period I prayed and prayed, but the heavens seemed to be brass. I felt as though God had disappeared and that I was all alone with my trial and burden. It was a dark night for my soul. I wrote my mother about the experience and will never forget her reply: "Son, there are many times when God withdraws to test your faith. He wants you to trust Him in the darkness. Now, son, reach up by faith in the fog, and you will find that His hand will be there." In tears I knelt by my bed and experienced an overwhelming sense of God's presence. Whether or not we sense and feel the presence of the Holy Spirit or of the holy angels, by faith we are certain God will never leave or forsake us.

About a week after my experience of seeing the wall of white stones, darkness fell upon me. I felt terrified and anxious all day and would shake uncontrollably because of an intense feeling of fear. I had great difficulty sleeping, and I could not wait for the dawn each day. Yet, dawn would not bring me peace. I still felt I was in darkness, even though the sun had risen in the sky. Most days during this period, I felt I was doing battle with, and facing an onslaught of, evil. I was emotionally, physically, and spiritually exhausted. I also felt I was barely hanging on each day. I was in despair and felt as if I may lose my mind.

After my illness, I completely surrendered my life to God. As part of my surrender and commitment, I developed a daily time with God. I would rise about an hour and a half before everyone in my house. I would sit at my counter, read my Bible or other faith strengthening books, journal, and pray. However, during the dark night of my soul in 2006, my kitchen counter became more of an altar, where I sobbed and cried out to God every morning. I just wanted it to stop. I wrestled with God and His Word. He unearthed and exposed deep lies and replaced them with His truth. Daily, God shaped me. My heart, my hurts, and the things that were not of Him became exposed. I would often remember things that were done to me and things that I had done to others. I prayed for and sought forgiveness on all sides.

During this dark period of time, I even had to let go of certain friends. They were not bad people or a bad influence. I knew how to let go of people who were a bad influence on me; but I found it much more difficult to let go of people who were a positive influence on me, and I grieved our lost friendship. They were good people and Christians, but they were people I relied on too much and gave too much authority in my life. I found myself seeking them all too often when I had a problem, and not going to God. I allowed them to influence me and direct me, instead of God and His Word. God is a jealous God, and He does not want other people or things placed in front of Him. I have since reconciled with these people, and our relationships are now in proper order, with God first.

Although horrific and painful, it was during this time my relationship with God grew the most. Even though I felt surrounded by darkness and all alone, I groped for God and continued to seek Him. I began to slowly learn I was not alone, abandoned, or rejected by God. He was with me and for me. I am free and forgiven. I am the daughter of the King who is worth fighting for.

While I had some friends stripped away, there were some I did keep. God gave me a good friend with whom I could honestly share my heart and experiences. She prayed for and encouraged me. She guided me to scripture and was not afraid to speak the truth in love to me when I needed someone to be direct. She never shrank from the truth of God's Word to spare my feelings or to placate me. She was more concerned with the state of my soul rather than offending me or worrying about losing our friendship. God was first, and she spoke His truth. She always pointed to God and His Word. That is a good friend.

I had another friend who knew I was struggling and would pray for me. One day she called me and said she put a letter in my mailbox for me. In the letter she told me how, when praying for me, she felt God wanted her to share certain scriptures with me. In the letter were all of the scriptures to which I had been clinging and in which I had placed hope during this dark time, plus a few bonus scriptures! It was such a beautiful confirmation I was seen and heard by God and that His Word is true.

During the dark night, I learned my relationship with Jesus Christ could no longer be a casual commitment. I had to truly decide:

Is He who He says He is; the Christ, the Son of God?
Is He truly Lord of my life?
Is He really worth giving up everything for?
Do I believe His Word?
Do I believe and understand His character?
Do I believe His promises?
Do I believe what He says about me: that I am chosen, saved, and free from sin, guilt, and shame?
Do I believe the old is truly gone and I am alive and new?

It is one thing to hear the Word of life and to read it, and yet another thing altogether to believe it and live it. It is about moving the seed of knowledge from your head to the soil of your heart where it can grow, bloom, and transform your being into whom God created you and purposed you to be. When moved to the rich soil of the heart and then watered by the Spirit, one can live out their days here on earth in faith, glorifying Him and knowing they will one day see Him face to face in eternity. The enemy has no hold.

Thankfully, during this extremely difficult time, God gave me two dreams to help me and give me direction.

In the first dream, I dreamt I was floating on my back in a large pool of water, and Jesus was with me. His hands were placed just below my back under the water.

When I reflected on the dream, it reminded me of when I taught my own children to float on their backs. They were so afraid I would let them sink. My hands would be placed under the water just beneath their backs. I would look into their worried but precious faces as they struggled and puffed air out of their mouths in case water got in. With all of my heart and my whole being, I just wanted them to relax and know how much I fiercely loved them. I wanted them to know I would never let them go or allow them to sink. I would be right there with them the whole time, holding them and teaching them. I wanted them to trust me.

In the second dream, I dreamt I was walking along, and Jesus was at my side. As we were walking, I asked Him, "How can you love someone so much, but not trust them?" When I asked this, I was referring to God.

I realized my core issue was I did not trust God. I felt rejected by Him, although I loved Him deeply.

# CHAPTER 7

## IT'S IN THE PAST

**Therefore, if anyone is in Christ, the new creation has come:**
**The old has gone, the new is here!**

2 Corinthians 5:17

There are many key events from my past that caused me to lose my trust in God and feel rejected by Him.

When I was about seven years old, I was horribly molested. I do not remember how I ended up in a strange man's car. I do not know how I got away. I do remember looking at the sky through the window of the car and crying out to God.

My teacher that same year ostracized me. I began to struggle in school because of what had happened to me. She regularly picked on me to answer questions, and when I got them wrong, which was most of the time, she would send me out of the classroom and into the hall, alone. Embarrassed, I would rise up from my desk. Ashamed, I would walk in front of the class to the door that led to the hallway. I would then spend most of the day in the hallway, alone. The class bully enjoyed giving me a hard time too.

Later that year, when I was still seven, my father was diagnosed with lymphoma. He was sick for seven years before he passed away. He was in and out of the hospital often and for long stays. He suffered greatly. I loved my father, and we were very close. I considered him my best friend. I prayed often for my father to be healed and felt deep sorrow on the day of his death. I was fourteen when he died, and I remember sitting on the side of my bed in tears and praying to God that if one day his death could be used to help someone else, then it would be okay. Yet I, nevertheless, felt the great void of losing him.

A few years prior to my father's death, his father died of the same disease. A few years after, my mother's father died of a heart condition. During this time, my great grandfather died as well from old age.

Around the time of my father's diagnosis, my mother developed a large brain tumor on her left frontal lobe. That area of the brain controls behavior, problem solving, judgement, and decision making, as well as emotional regulation. It is the "control panel" of our personality. Her tumor went undiagnosed for more than 15 years, until I was 25 years old. When it was finally diagnosed and removed, the damage had already been substantial; and as a result, she has frontal lobe syndrome.

While growing up, because of the large tumor growing in her brain, of which we were then unaware, my mother's emotions and behavior were often erratic and extreme. I never knew what to expect. Her words and actions were sometimes contradictory and confusing. For example, I was told I was loved, but then I was told I wasn't doing enough. I was threatened, as a teenager, to be kicked out of the house. I was told how great it was to have a daughter, but in various other ways, I was told I was not wanted. I was told I looked pretty, but then was told I was fat and had a big butt. My dreams and aspirations were discouraged for nonsensical reasons. I was often awakened in the middle of the night for no apparent reason. My mother would turn on my lights and call out my name, startle me, and then slam the door shut. I did not know what to expect or believe. One day, I just stopped believing anything positive. The negative actions and language coming from my mother carried a profound weight and force that deeply affected me. The negative far outweighed the positive, especially as her tumor grew.

Another dynamic that made the situation with my mother so difficult and exasperating appeared when she somehow managed to maintain and keep control in front of neighbors, church members, extended family, and certainly, my father. However, she would lose control at home when only her kids were around. When someone else was around or we were in public, the façade sprang up. She was like two very different people. These experiences and situations with my mother caused me to feel defeated and hopeless, like I could not do anything right. I wondered what was so wrong with me that my mother treated me so differently than others. I felt as though something bad may happen to me at any moment, and I was always on edge.

Prior to my father's death, when family and friends did see her erratic emotions and odd behavior, they attributed it to having a sick husband and small children. After my father's death, they attributed her emotions and behavior to having lost her husband and having teenagers. Because of the tumor in her brain, though, and her inability to control herself at times, I can surmise it must have taken her great strength and concentration to hold it together when she was around others and, unfortunately, a welcome relief to her when she was outside the presence of others, besides her children. Sadly, she was misdiagnosed, and she suffered for many years.

Before her tumor, though, when she was younger, some of her friends have described her as loving, free spirited, creative, the first to make a meal or be there when someone was going through a hard time, and a joy to be around. She was silly and full of laughter. My mother was a dramatic extrovert who wanted to have fun. Both she and my father were deeply in love with one another. I am thankful I was able to witness that deep love. My mother was more than an excellent caregiver for my father. I know it must have taken great energy to be positive and strong for him, even though she, herself, was suffering as well.

I want to preface this next paragraph by saying I deeply love my brother, care for him, and forgive him. We were young when these things happened. He is a different person now, and I am too.

While I was young, from early childhood until about the time my father passed, my brother was often cruel to me. We were often left alone, because my mother was usually at the hospital with my father. She was afraid to leave his side. Not only were those times painful, but when my mother was home, I would often call to her for help; and while she heard me and knew what was going on, she ignored me and my cries for help. I was angrier with my mother for not protecting me than I was at my brother for mistreating me. Like me, though, he too had his own struggles, trauma, and negative life events. Everyone under our roof had struggles, trauma, and negative life events. Our family had broken down, and there was little control in our home.

Outside the home, I was sometimes bullied and made fun of as well. This occurred until I was in my early teens, until I lost my awkwardness. I was very tall when I was young, taller than most everyone my age, and I looked boyish. I had a friend tell me her mother did not want her to be friends with me anymore because of the way I looked. Once, I was even taunted by a large group of people who chanted at me and made fun of my body.

All was not horribly lost. I was not void of friends. I did have a few good friends who are still my friends to this day. Our home was not always dark. We did have good times too, but not enough to keep me from losing trust in God.

During the years of 1976 and 1977, when I was ten and eleven years old, our community lived in fear and suffered greatly. Those years marked the time when four children from our community were abducted and murdered at separate times by a man known as the Oakland County Child Killer. We were all terrified to play outside or walk to a friend's house. The last victim, Timothy, was a friend of my brother. They played baseball together. Everyone prayed vehemently for his return. I remember the morning my mother told me they had found Timothy's body in the snow. I was sitting at the table eating my breakfast, and I felt the deep crushing heartache of unanswered prayer.

My high school years, after my father's passing, were punctuated with more death, as I lost several classmates and friends to car accidents and illness.

As a result of all of the negativity in my young life, I did not feel very welcome in the world. I felt there was nowhere safe for me. Not only did I feel unprotected, but I felt unworthy of protection or that I was not worth standing up for. I felt as though I had no voice and felt I really did not matter. I had lost hope and had no sense of purpose.

I bundled all of these experiences with many more and concluded God must not love me and must have rejected me. I viewed Him as a big bully in the sky. I projected my earthly experiences with human beings onto God and who I thought He was and what I thought He must be like. I looked around at all I had been through at my young age and thought He surely must not exist. If He did, why should I trust Him?

My heart began to harden. I became angry and bitter, wild and promiscuous. I abused drugs and alcohol. I struggled with an eating disorder (sometimes still do). I thought often of ending my life. I simply felt I could not take the pain anymore. I surrounded myself with people who were a bad influence. In turn, I was a bad influence on others. I made poor decisions. I moved away from home when I was nineteen. I thought a new start in a different state, far away from home, would help, but my behavior followed me. I just changed locations.

One night, when I was 21, I was date raped. There were people in the other room who heard what was going on, but they did nothing. A week later, after experiencing the death of another family member, adding to the pain from being raped, I went out into the night to kill the pain with alcohol. I got into a fight with a police officer who was just trying to get me home safely. I ended up staying the night in jail, where a prostitute laughed at me all night. I had hit bottom.

A few days later, after I had sobered up, while walking down the road, coming home from the grocery store, I realized I hated my life. I was not going anywhere, and everything seemed to be a mess. I again felt hopeless. I was still at the very bottom of the pit, feeling completely helpless. In that moment, though, I decided to do something I had not done in years. I turned to God. After going my own way and making a giant mess of things, I prayed to Him. Praying was something I had not done in years, let alone believe in God or believe He would even hear me. I said, "God, I am doing a very poor job with my life. I have made a mess of it. I am ready for whom You want me to be with." In the very deep recesses of my heart, I wanted God to change my life.

At that moment, I felt the very Presence of God and that He was actually listening to me. I felt hopeful and determined after praying. I decided it was time to take personal responsibility for my actions and behavior and not act like a victim. There was no excuse to do what I had been doing, simply because of all the things I went through. I resolved to get back into college. I resolved to quit doing drugs and to drink in moderation. I quit my job and cut off the people who were a bad influence.

I met the man who would later become my husband, not long after that prayer, and we started going to church together, which was something else I had not done in years. I had been hurt by the church on more than several occasions and was skeptical of Christians, but I was willing to try again.

Although I changed many things in my life, and the years moved on, my heart and mind still needed much work.

When I had a second chance at life, after being healed from lymphoma, and later after God did the healing miracle with the blood clot, I strove for forgiveness. Being healed and knowing I was free and forgiven, I decided to not hold people captive in unforgiveness. Many of my own personal experiences, including what others did or said to me, now seemed unimportant. Truly, it all did not matter anymore.

Those experiences, whether traumatic or petty, pale in comparison when you realize one day we will all stand in the Presence of God and give an accounting of our lives. In light of all the ways God showed Himself to me during my illness, holding onto anger and bitterness seemed unimportant and draining. I wanted to be free of those debilitating emotions.

I recognized I harbored a lot of anger and bitterness toward my mother, and it was affecting my marriage and my ability to be a good mother. As an adult, I could understand, have compassion, and reconcile she was ill. Her behavior towards me was not her fault, but the child in me was hurt and scarred. Children basically want four things: "acceptance, focused attention, guidance, and protection." [1] I felt void of a lot these things, and I was angry and bitter. I prayed to God to help me forgive my mother. I was willing to forgive her, but I did not know how. I also realized I had been angry at her for so long, and I had no other narrative in my head and heart to pull from. I was used to being angry and bitter. Forgiving and loving seemed very difficult and far off. The anger and bitterness seemed easier and more comfortable. Forgiving and loving seemed like a difficult, scary challenge that made me feel vulnerable. However, God gave me a dream on the night I truly desired and asked for forgiveness for us both. I wanted us to be free. I asked Him for His help, and He gave it to me.

I dreamt I was at my grandmother's (my mother's mom) house. My grandmother's house was my safe place growing up. Her house was clean and smelled good. She had a beautiful garden. She was a ceramicist and watercolorist. We would paint together or make pottery out of clay at her kitchen table. Her home felt so peaceful. My grandmother had passed away a few years earlier, but I saw her in this dream.

The dream felt so real. My grandmother appeared before me and called my name. She said, "Kristin, look at your mother." I turned and looked at my mother and saw her just as I saw her at that point in my life. As I looked at her, I felt all of the anger and bitterness. Then my grandmother said to me, "I want you to look at your mother again." I turned and looked at my mother again, and she turned into the mother I knew when I was five years old. When you are little, your mother is beautiful. When you are little, your mother hangs the moon. She is great, and your love for her is deep. My grandmother then said to me, "This is who God intended your mother to be. This is how she will look when you see her in heaven one day."

When I woke, I felt a deep feeling of forgiveness for my mother, and the anger and bitterness had evaporated. I really understood more deeply it was not my mother with whom I had been struggling. I had been struggling with an unseen illness, and the effects of that illness, and not whom my mother truly was. I even had a desire to call my mother, which I had never had in the past. I called rarely and out of obligation, not devotion. However, when I called my mother this time, I heard the words I had been longing to hear my whole life. She said, "Kristin, I want to tell you what a good job you are doing. You are a good wife and a good mother. Your kids are wonderful, and you married a good man. You are a great artist, and I am so proud of you." I hung up the phone and just sobbed. I felt the hardness of my heart crack and the flood of forgiveness pour in. How great is God! I realized my mother had been telling me these things before, but I had stopped hearing and believing them, because they were mixed in with all the negative comments. My heart had become hard, my eyes had become dark, and my ears had closed to anything good, but God changed me.

Sometimes forgiveness comes in layers, because you really do not know how deep those wounds are that need healing. Forgiveness with my mom was like that. It came in layers, after the initial crack in my heart.

For example, she was in the hospital not long ago, and I went to visit her. While I was there, a doctor came in and began asking a lot of questions my mom could not answer. When I saw she could not answer, she gave me permission to answer for her. I then apologized to my mother, because I had to tell the doctor about some of her behavior while I was growing up. I told her it was not to hurt her, but to answer the doctor's questions so he could help. I spoke as kindly, as gently, and as generically as I could, because I did not want to hurt my mother after all she has been through. After I gave the doctor two examples of her behavior that I thought may help, my mother said, with a pained look on her face to the doctor and myself, "I always knew what was the right thing to do, but I could never make myself do it." I saw at that moment how she was at war within herself. I saw how it must have hurt her heart, mind, and soul to do and say some of the things she did and not be able to help or stop herself.

Another moment of forgiveness came on my birthday a few years ago. My mother called me to wish me a happy birthday, which was a rarity. After I left home, when I was 19, birthdays would come and go without her acknowledging them. Prior to her diagnosis, no acknowledgement of my birthday deeply hurt, but afterward, I understood why. When she would remember, it was a gift. But this particular year she called me to wish me a happy birthday. She told me she was sad not to be with me and wished we could have coffee together. My mother told me she decided she would have coffee with me anyway. She proceeded to tell me she dressed in all purple, because I liked purple, and even had on a purple hat. She decided to decorate the outside of her hat by lining it with birthday candles. She then took a framed picture of me and walked to the coffee shop near her apartment. She ordered two coffees, one for me and one for her. She sat down at a table and placed my picture in the frame on the table. She put the cup of coffee by it. My mother then told me that, shortly thereafter, the manager of the store approached her and asked her what she was doing. She told the manager she was having a birthday cup of coffee with her daughter, like it was completely natural and like he was clueless and should have understood exactly what she was doing.

My heart just soared. I felt so much joy and happiness. She was celebrating me and honoring me the best and only way she knew how. I felt so very loved.

One of my uncles told me that when you realize your parents only did the best they were capable of doing at the time and have peace with that, then you can begin healing. My mother did the very best she could.

There were other moments of forgiveness along the way, and I treasured and thanked God for each one, grateful for the freedom for us both.

So, ask God to help you forgive if you are unable.

As time moved on, around 10 years ago, I became aware that my mind, like my heart, also needed a lot of work. I had a continual wheel of self-hatred spinning in my head. I realized no one was around to verbally beat me up, so I beat myself up. I was confirming over and over all of the hurtful things said to me in my early years, as well as reliving all of the bad things I had done or were done to me. I had so much pain, guilt, and shame burdening me.

Slowly, however, I began to spend more daily time with God and apply His Word to my life. It was toward the end of my dark night that my false narrative of self-hatred began to fade into silence. It changed one day when I was visiting a church and God spoke to me through the pastor. God interrupted my narrative of self-hatred and said to me, "You have become what you thought. Now become who I say you are. Believe My words. Accept and agree with My purpose for you and who I say you are." That moment was pivotal. Not only did I decide to apply God's truth to my life, I decided to fully believe it. I decided to believe Him and not man, or my own misunderstandings, but to work toward trusting Him.

Around the same time, I remember reading the scripture found in Colossians 1:17, "In him all things hold together." I thought if Jesus holds all things together, He could hold me together too.

Gradually, the depression and anxiety of the dark night began to lift. God sorted through all of my distorted thoughts and false narratives I had formed about Him and myself. This took time, though. It took years. I am still a work in progress. We looked at the painful parts of my life together, God and I; and I sought healing, peace, and forgiveness not only for others, but for the most difficult person to forgive, myself. Thankfully, He began to breathe His truth into the broken pieces of my life, heart, and mind, mending them together with His love and truth. God restored me and slowly healed my heart and my mind. At that point in time, I began to learn who God is, His character, and what His promises are, and who I am in Him.

I also came to understand the meaning of the dream He gave me. He would not let me sink. He loves me. I am His child. I was never alone. God did not forsake me. He did not let go of me. He is with me, and the Holy Spirit is inside of me. He has good for me, and I can trust Him. Before, I was measuring God and perceiving God through the eyes of someone hurt by sinful man in a fallen world. God did not hurt me. 1 John 4:8 says, "God is love." Man stepped away from God and hurt me, and I hurt myself. Just because I went through difficult times and made poor choices did not mean God was not present with me or did not love me. At one point, my circumstances and my own actions and wrongful beliefs caused me to think He did not exist, but now I know He loves me and has been present with me my whole life. God made a way for me through Jesus, and I chose that way. Now I look to, and rely on, God's Word for who He is and who I am in Him.

One more thing regarding my past.

Solomon wrote, "Promise me, O women of Jerusalem, not to awaken love until the time is right" (Song of Solomon NLT 8:4).

These are truly wise words.

One of the sweetest messages of love from God was one He gave me for an orphan who lives halfway around the world from me. A friend of mine asked me to create a piece of art as a gift for one of the orphans she would be visiting in Romania.

These particular orphans were girls about to enter society as adults. Often times, the majority of them fall into prostitution, because they are unable to find employment.

As I created the piece of art, I heard God say, "You are a child of beauty, created by Me and for Me, fearfully and wonderfully made, not someone to be climbed and conquered, but someone to be loved and looked upon with awe and beauty." I believe this message applies to all.

Our culture today tells us so many lies regarding sex. It was not created as a means to get attention, fill a void, be glamorous, or have power over others. It was not meant to harm and enslave others. These things break apart the soul. Sex is to mirror God's uniting and deep love for and with us. It mirrors His sacrificial love. It is sacred, holy, worshipful, and to be celebrated. It is meant for His timing and not ours.

Before my husband and I were married, we got pregnant. It was an unhealthy pregnancy. I was doubled over in severe pain and could not stand upright. My belly was abnormally swollen with an unusual amount of excess amniotic fluid, and I was bleeding on and off. With a sorrowful and concerned look on his face, my doctor told me I would miscarry at some point, but he did not know when. He said even if I went on bed rest, it was inevitable. For my health, he advised I not wait to miscarry, but have an abortion. He thought both the physical and emotional pain would be worse the longer I waited. Conflicted, and after much consideration, we decided to listen to the doctor and do as he said.

What some doctors may not tell you, what our culture certainly will not tell you, but what I will tell you, is that when you have an abortion, your heart and soul are shattered into a million pieces. You will endure a great amount of emotional pain as the result of your choice. You remember the month or day you got pregnant. You remember the month or day they would have been born. Years will pass, but you still remember and mourn. What was once a part of you, one with you, and connected to you, was ripped away, leaving a great void. You grieve and despise yourself, because you stopped a beating heart. Although the medical reasoning was logical, I could not emotionally reconcile what I had done.

My choice became an unmarked grave that left a scar on my heart that was crying out to be named. It was a grave dug by my own hand. You think abortion is silent, but it is a pain that echoes in your heart, mind, and soul. My choice became an obstacle to fully receiving God's grace. Yet, grace is given to me; and it is the only thing that has healed my heart, mind, and soul. Although I am certainly not deserving of it, grace has given me peace. It is given to me, and I receive it with both hands, gratefully outstretched and open. "Therefore, there is now no condemnation for those who are in Christ Jesus." ( Romans 8:1)

God's love moves mountains and fills voids. His love transforms and inspires. We are hesitant to draw near to it once we recognize our own fallen selves, but He does not despise what He has created. He gives us plenty of space for repentance. He does not force us, but in true power, His love waits patiently for us and welcomes us in. It beckons us close, then enfolds us and covers us. His love transforms us into who we are truly meant to be. We are free.

Carl Jung was once quoted, "The world will ask you who you are, and if you do not know, the world will tell you."

Many people say the Bible is just a collection of stories written long ago and irrelevant. Let me be crystal clear. I did not find truth, healing, peace, identity, belongingness, or purpose in the world. I found those things in God's Word, the Bible, and by building a relationship with Him. The One who created the heavens and earth and created me knows who and whose I am. He calls me beloved and His child. He knows me, and He knows my purpose. He knows you and calls you too.

# CHAPTER 8

## MY PURPOSE

**Those who sow with tears will reap with songs of joy.**

Psalm 126:5

I am so very humbled and in awe of God and how He has a purpose and plan for someone with a past like mine. Great is His mercy and transformative power! It deeply moves my heart to think of His great and merciful love for us all, but that is God's character. He is the one who lifts us out of the pit. He "bestow[s] on [us] a crown of beauty instead of ashes, the oil of joy instead of mourning, and a garment of praise instead of a spirit of despair. They will be called oaks of righteousness, a planting of the Lord for the display of his splendor." (Isaiah 61:3) It gives Him pleasure to do so!

I have always loved creating. I pursued my passion in college, although not the traditional student, and earned a Bachelor of Fine Arts degree with a concentration in painting from Georgia State University. My art, though, did not always look as it does now.

Prior to becoming ill in 2003, I was self-employed and had my own business doing interior and exterior color consulting as well as faux finishes and murals. I also sold some of my art by word of mouth, and I had a couple of pieces in a local gallery. My art was often dark, angry charcoal drawings; although I sometimes created large, colorful landscapes or figures using oil paint.

When I became ill, I could no longer use charcoal, oil paints, or the mediums I had used to create faux finishes and murals, because the fumes and other irritants made it difficult for me to breathe. I had to completely change everything. I was very ill for quite some time and suffered many side effects from the chemotherapy and radiation. It took years to recover. I had a nice business for myself prior to becoming ill, but afterward, I had to let all of it go.

Meanwhile, I had completely surrendered my life to God; and I wanted to glorify Him with my work, but I really did not know what that looked like. Gradually over time, I learned to listen to His Holy Spirit and be guided by Him. Initially, God gave me an image with one little word in a dream. The image was in black and white. It was a cross, and the word "hope" was attached to it. Over time, I learned to trust God through the creative process. I learned, sometimes reluctantly, to create as I felt He was instructing me. As I began to trust Him more, He, in turn, entrusted me with more images and more words. While He initially gave me images through dreams and visions in black and white, He later reintroduced color. Similarly, while He had begun with one word, He later increased the messages with scripture; then poetry; then prayers, with His own answer to each prayer; and then personal messages for whomever I was creating the piece of art.

I gave many of my paintings, which included scripture, poetry, and messages on the backs of each piece or written in a letter, as gifts to people. Interestingly, God not only had me create for people I loved and for whom I was grateful, but He had me create for people with whom I had contention or lingering unforgiveness. He had me give the art to them as a gift. He impressed upon me He did not pick and choose his children. He died for all, and His gift of grace is for all. Therefore, I should not pick and choose either. While I created for this latter group of people, I learned so much about each person and myself. My heart often broke for them and swelled with love, after which I found forgiveness and compassion. I began to see them through God's eyes and also see my own shortcomings and wounds that had been reopened. As a result, I asked God to heal them. I am so very grateful to God for those opportunities.

There came a time after all of my treatments and my husband's three knee surgeries when our family was struggling financially. Both my husband and I are self-employed. After the economy crashed in 2008, and the recession that followed, we had a pile of medical bills, a child headed to college, and another soon to follow. We struggled to get by. Even though I felt called to paint and it was my passion, I had to set it aside.

I said to God, "God, I cannot stay home and paint anymore. Our family needs help." After much prayer, I began to look for a job. I thankfully was able to find one in an assisted living home. I had not worked for anyone in over ten years. I thought I would work at the assisted living home while I continued to look for a job elsewhere that was more in my field.

After working at the assisted living home for a while, our family structure changed again. My father-in-law's cancer had progressed to where he was in the final weeks of his life.

My father-in-law had been sick with cancer for fifteen years. Most people who had the same illness lasted a maximum of eleven years. My father-in-law was a tough man, a man's man. He had lived a very rough life. My mother-in-law's stead-fast prayer for her husband was that the Lord would grant him mercy. My sister-in-law and brother-in-law were helping to care for him during these final days when they gave us a call to let us know how serious it had become.

My husband and I made the drive to West Tennessee while our children stayed home. We did not know what to ex-pect. It was a Wednesday when we arrived. My father-in-law was at home, lying in a hospital bed in the family room. He wanted to die at home. He was clearly going to pass soon.

Thursday afternoon, we thought he was dying. He was struggling to breathe. He wanted us to call our children so he could tell them he loved them and say goodbye. There were several other people he wanted us to help him call so he could say goodbye to them as well. We could see and feel my father-in-law was very frightened. We encouraged him to go to Jesus and assured him we would all be okay. We told him it was not "Goodbye," but "See you later," and we would see him in heaven one day. His wife asked if he could hear Jesus calling to him, and he said he could; but we could see he was still so very fright-ened. I asked my father-in-law to say hello to my dad when he got to heaven and to please tell him I loved him. Even though they had never met, I told my father-in-law how much he would like my dad. Soon, thereafter, my father-in-law fell asleep. We thought he would pass that night.

Friday morning came, and my father-in-law had not passed. In his weakest moments, he was still strong and determined. We could tell he wanted to see his grandchildren one more time. My husband and I decided he should drive back home and get our children so they could come say goodbye to their grandfather in person. My husband drove one, eleven-hour roundtrip to get our children there as soon as possible.

Later that afternoon, after my husband had left on his road trip, I was in the family room with my father-in-law. I was sitting on the couch keeping watch when he awoke and held out his hand to me. I went over to him, shocked he was awake. He still looked frightened, worried, and concerned. He asked me to get his wife. Once again, the two of us encouraged him to go to Jesus and re-assured him we would all be okay and it was not "Goodbye," but "See you later."

As we sat with him, and as his fear remained, I asked him, "What is wrong? You seem so worried and afraid." In the most pitiful voice, he cried out, "God hates me, because I am bad!" I told him that is a LIE of the evil one and to not listen. Then Psalm 27:10 popped in my head, "Though your parents may reject you, I the Lord will receive you." I spoke these words and a flood of tears came as he just sobbed. After speaking the scripture, I recalled how my father-in-law had felt rejected by his own father as a child and was often treated poorly.

I assured my father-in-law his heavenly Father was nothing like his earthly father. His wife and I shared scripture with him and told him about the love of God. Jesus died for ALL, not some, but ALL. We told him how we all "fall short of the glory of God" (Romans 3:23), and how the apostle Paul was a murderer of Christians, but God used him to spread the Gospel and write almost half of the New Testament. We reminded him of Peter, who denied Jesus when close enough to hear, but Jesus still forgave and loved him. Jesus built His church on Peter. We poured out as much scripture as we could to assure him he was worthy of Christ's love. He was not rejected, but accepted and loved by God. We then asked him if he wanted to receive Jesus as his Lord and Savior. He said, "Yes," and we then prayed with him. He, once again, fell asleep shortly thereafter. I called my husband to tell him the good news, and our whole family rejoiced.

Early Saturday at 1:00 a.m., my husband arrived with our children, and my father-in-law woke up again. This time he truly awoke. We could see a great transformation in him. Indeed, he was a new creation (2 Corinthians 5:17). He was full of peace and a child-like joy. He smiled and beamed. He was radiant.

We all told him we loved him and were so happy that he accepted Christ. He wanted to make sure all of us knew Jesus too, and we all confirmed to him we did. Suddenly, he got a dark, somber look and said in a low voice, "I didn't want to go to that other place." We were all quiet. We knew what he meant. He did not want to go to hell. He continued, "They had a rope tied around me, and they were trying to pull me into the other place, but a man came and helped me." I then asked my father-in-law if Jesus had come to help him; but he said, "No. Your father came to help me; and he is standing right over there, and he says, 'I love you Kristin'."

I just sobbed. I remembered my prayer from when I was fourteen years old, right after my father had passed. God had used my father's death to help someone. My father-in-law's soul was saved. My father helped pull my father-in-law out of the pit of hell. God had just given me some understanding, and I praised Him. I also realized that throughout the difficulties of my life, God had actually placed my father in the most powerful place possible. God placed my father in heaven to intercede on my behalf and on behalf of others. We truly cannot conceive or understand God's plans.

A moment later, after my father-in-law spoke those words regarding my father helping him, he looked at me and said, "I have a message for you." I asked, "What is the message?" He started to speak, but we could not hear him, because he was speaking softly and reverently. My brother-in-law said, "Speak up, we can't hear you." Then my father-in-law sat up, which he had not done in several days, and looked right at me and loudly, with authority, said, "I am speaking for Jesus now. He is standing right over there. He wants you to paint Kristin." Once again, I just sobbed. I got on my face and said "Yes." Then my father-in-law said, "I am standing in heaven now. It won't be long now." He was so excited. All of his fear and anxiety had disappeared and was replaced with joy and confidence. Excitedly he said, "I am getting ready to get on up out of this place!"

He gathered us around him and prayed for our whole family. He said many other wonderful things. All of us were so full of joy. Then he asked me, "If it is at all possible, will you wait with me until I go?" I said, "Yes." Then he fell asleep again. I held his hand and barely left his side. When he would occasionally wake, our family would read scripture to him. He was full of so many beautiful questions about the Lord and His Word. We all did our best to explain what we could to him. Surrounded by most of his family, my father-in-law passed that Tuesday afternoon.

A short time after he passed, I started getting images in dreams for me to paint. I kept, and still keep, a sketchbook by my bed to sketch what God gives me. I get up and sketch during the night or first thing in the morning. During the creative process, I started receiving, and still receive, words of love and encouragement or prayers to accompany each image.

May I be faithful to create and pass on each image and word the Lord gives me. Amen.

As a final thought in this chapter, I can confirm that the spirit of rejection is an evil force that can deafen our ears and blind our eyes to the love of God that is in Christ Jesus. Christ Himself faced rejection while here on this earth. Isaiah 53:3 says, "He was despised and rejected by men, a man of sorrows, and familiar with suffering. Like one from whom men hide their faces, he was despised, and we esteemed him not." In Luke Chapter 4, it says Jesus was rejected in His hometown, and His very own church even tried to throw Him off a cliff. He was rejected by the religious leaders in Jerusalem, and they conspired to take His life. John, Chapter 7, says that His own brothers did not believe Him. Jesus was even abandoned and rejected by His closest friends in the hour of His greatest need, as even Peter three times denied knowing Jesus. Sadly, today, Jesus is still being rejected, but His arms are always open wide to receive us. He will even pursue us to the gates of hell to bring us to His loving embrace.

I implore you to set aside what man has said and done to you. Look to God's Word, and learn the truth about yourself. Let Him speak to your heart and mind. Allow Him to heal them, and walk in His freedom.

**Be transformed by the renewing of your mind.**

Romans 12:2

# CHAPTER 9

## DREAMS AND VISIONS

**I will pour out my Spirit on all people. Your sons and
daughters will prophesy, your young men will see visions,
your old men will dream dreams.**

Joel 2:28 and Acts 2:17

In this chapter, I want to share some of the dreams and often detailed visions I have had over the years. While many of
these dreams concern the church, I also pray these dreams and
visions help enlighten, strengthen, and encourage you.

I had a dream about a large procession of people who were being led into a great city by Jesus Christ. The city was surrounded by a great wall. They were all happy, full of joy, and celebrating. There were others who looked on and wanted to join the
procession. They were welcome to join and invited to join, but
they hesitated. Once the procession had finished entering the
great city, the doors of the city slammed shut. The people who
wanted to join but had hesitated could not get in. The door
had been shut, and the time to enter had passed. Then a great
wind came, and they were swept away into the sky.

I had a dream where I was in a public school with many other people. We all had what looked like cardboard wicks, like
candles in our hands. We were all in a line, and we dipped our
"wicks" into an oil that had a fragrance to it. We then lit the
wicks, our "candles," after they had been dipped into the oil. We
walked through the school and prayed while holding our candles, because the school was dark. Darkness had descended on
the public school, and our candles provided the only light. We
walked around the inside of the school and prayed over all of
the classrooms. We invited the Lord to come in and asked for

His protection over the children and that they would know Him. Outside of the school, however, there were many people who did not understand what we were doing, and they were angry about it. They did not want us to pray, simply because they did not understand. We were inviting the Lord into the schools. We were inviting His Presence and protection. From the outside, unbelievers were angry and mad, simply because they did not know God. From the inside, we were doing the most important and powerful thing possible to protect our children, inviting the Lord back in to the school. The Lord and prayer are our greatest protection; our greatest covering over our children.

I had a dream where I was shown the back of Jesus. He was facing away from me, and I could see the back of His crown, hair, and robe. I asked, "Lord, what is this?" He answered, "How do you walk behind a King?"

I had a dream for the church, generally, that is, the body of believers regardless of any denomination. I dreamt I was climbing up a rock face on the side of a mountain. I was clinging to the side of the mountain, and when I looked down, I saw a rushing river below me. In the river, I saw someone being swept away in the current, and I wanted to save them. I then looked to the top of the mountain and saw a great Light. In that Light, I saw Jesus. I again wanted to jump in and pull the person to the mountain, but I heard the Lord say, "There is a food shortage." I realized if I pulled the person to safety, they would, nevertheless, starve.

Know His Word. His Word is food for the soul.

I had a dream about Mary, the blessed mother of Jesus. She was very pregnant, and she was getting ready to mount a donkey. She had one foot in the stirrup, preparing to hoist her very pregnant body up and onto the donkey. She said, "Well, here we go!" I could see she had a little sense of humor about it. Then I heard the Lord say, "She did all that she could."

I had another dream for the church. I dreamt of a bride who was getting ready in a bridal suite. She was beautiful and radiant and her bridesmaids were with her. The bridesmaids, though, were grumbling against the bride. They were saying bad things about her, right there in the bridal suite in her presence while she was getting ready for her time to walk down the aisle.

I had a dream for the church. I dreamt I was walking along a sidewalk and came to the location of the church where I attended, but it was now a greenspace. As I stood there looking, a couple came to me and said, "We used to go there." I looked further and saw a long row of churches, and they were all in various states of disrepair and barely able to stay open. They were once large, thriving churches, but fell into disrepair, with only a few or no one attending. Some, like the church I attended, had been mowed down. I then walked across the street and saw a large, deep well. It had been sealed with a great metal seal. Suddenly, a woman approached on an excavator. There were small children riding along on the excavator, and I perceived them as the next generation. The woman said, "We have to dig deep." Then she began to pull the great metal seal off the well.

Lord, may the next generation know, love, and choose you. May they know Your Word. Your Word says we are always one generation away from being lost.

I had another dream for the church. I dreamt of the Lord, and He was asking, "Why would you not pray for someone?" I then perceived the lack of prayer had to do with disunity in the church and among believers. When we have contention or unforgiveness, or when we grumble against one another or the church, we withdraw prayer. Sometimes, we even withdraw prayer from our own family members with whom we may have contention or unforgiveness. I also perceived a lack of prayer for unbelievers in the church.

I had a vision of a large body of water with many people standing in it. Then I heard the Lord say, "If we all stand in the same waters, are we not one? Are we not joined by the water? Does it not flow through all? We are united in one Spirit. Can the water just dry up in one spot where someone is standing? No. Allow My great work and Spirit to work in others' lives too. Know they are being transformed too. Know My Spirit is at work in them, changing them in My perfect timing. You cannot say, 'They are not in the river with me.' But they are in that river and are under My grace, and I am working in them, just as I am working in you. All of those in the water need Me too. Some know to bend and drink. Others stand in the water and are parched. They are learning to bend and drink."

I had a dream for the church. I dreamt I was sitting in the pews in the sanctuary of a church with many other people, and we were listening to three types of worship and watching as different people came up to worship. The first group of people to worship were just trying to be entertaining and funny. Their hearts were not really in the worship, because they were just focused on entertaining and pleasing the people in the audience, not actually worshiping God. While they were performing, some of the people who were sitting in the pews got up and left.

Then the next group of people came up to worship. They were trying to worship and were focused not only on worship, but also on entertaining as well, and their hearts were not fully in it. As I watched and listened, more people who were sitting in the pews got up and left.

While I was waiting and preparing to listen to the third group of worshipers, I could hear them practicing, but they were not yet present in the sanctuary. They were getting ready and preparing to come in. They sounded heavenly and beautiful. They worshiped in Spirit and in truth. Their hearts were in it, and they were prepared. While I was waiting for them to come in, many more people who were sitting in the pews left, and more were getting ready to leave.

While I was sitting and waiting for the worshipers, I heard a woman speaking from outside the sanctuary. I looked to my right and saw an open door to another room. Inside the room were a man and a woman who were speaking ugly things about the worshipers and the church as a whole. Their conversation was about culture, race, and gender related issues that divide us, things they believed and had been taught in today's society. They were murmuring about a misperception they had been taught and had found its way into the church. They spoke in an ugly tone about how they view the church as a whole and the individual members of the church. Their misperception involved comparing one church to another church based upon where the church was located and who its members were. It was only a misperception these people had and not truth; but they believed it all and brought their own thoughts, perceptions, and cultural beliefs into the church. I told them to be quiet; we could hear them. Then I shut the door. I saw how this thought process created disunity in the church.

Meanwhile, more people were getting up from the pews and leaving. I then asked God why everyone was leaving. He said, "Because My Word is not being spoken." Then I too left, because the Word of God was not being spoken.

I had a dream in which I heard God say, "Mary rejoiced, and look at all that came through her." Then God impressed upon me that Mary's first response, when the angel Gabriel visited her and told her she would conceive Jesus by the Holy Spirit, was to rejoice. She felt neither fear nor shame of her circumstances or what was going to happen to her. She simply rejoiced for the moment and the saving of many for the future.

I had a dream of someone speaking in tongues. In the dream, someone else said, "You must have an interpreter if there are tongues. What did they say?" Then someone else spoke up and said, "They spoke about pride." In the dream, I then perceived pride in the church in general. The source of pride was rejecting spiritual gifts that people had, or rejecting people who they felt did not fit or belong in the church.

I had a dream where I was in a public place. It was either a school or business and was crowded with of people. All of a sudden, a foreign army came. They meant to invade, occupy, and change our way of life. They were rounding us up to kill us. The Spirit of God came upon me, and as I moved through the compacted, panicked crowd, I asked people if they wanted to receive Jesus Christ as their Lord and Savior. If they did, I prayed with them. Some people came, and I laid hands on them and prayed with them to receive Christ. As soon as they did, they felt a peace, became calm, and experienced an immediate transformation in their hearts and minds. I could actually see the difference. Then, the people who accepted Christ asked, "Why did I not receive Him sooner?" I then thought, "Why did I not tell them sooner?"

I had a dream of Mary, the blessed mother of Jesus. In the dream she was so very beautiful. She held out her hand and said, "Give it to me." I had this yucky, dirty thing in my hand, and she wanted it. I was hesitant to give it to her, because I did not want my dirty, soiled things to get on her. Reluctantly, I gave it to her, and immediately I wanted to take it back. She said, "You can't take it back now that you have given it to me." When I awoke from the dream, I considered how, as a mother, I would do anything to take away my child's hurt or pain so they would not have to suffer.

I had a dream of a deep and narrow path, dug like a canyon or deep crevasse, and there was a giant heart in the sky above the path. The heart represented God leading in love, and the path was made by God's hand, a passageway. The heart is His banner of love that flies over the path, which has been dug by water. The ledges are too steep to climb, but whoever is on the path is protected by great rock walls.

I had a dream of people in need, including some who were sick. I walked to each person to ask and find what was wrong. Each person said their needs were not being met. They only received something small and little, which in no way met their needs. One woman had cancer, and she said, "I only received this little container of milk." In the dream, I perceived as Christians, followers of Jesus Christ, we need to be generous with God's Word for lifting and encouraging others. I also perceived we, as Christians, need to claim God's healing power and to pray for others. God has given us so much spiritual authority. In my dream, I saw how the church was failing to serve others in need.

In a dream, I heard the words "Purple Jesus." I then perceived how Christ is sometimes viewed. We only see the surface of Him, what is on the outside. Do we really know Him and His heart? It is like only seeing someone's skin color and not really seeing them or knowing them, who they are on the inside and what their heart is like. In the same way, people make general assumptions about Christ without truly knowing who He is, just like people make general assumptions about others without truly knowing who they are. He wants you to know Him more.

In a dream, I heard the Lord speak, "My mother watched" (meaning that Mary watched Jesus die).

I had a dream that evil in this world had increased, but did not look how I thought it should look. Yes, obvious evil increased, like the killing of people, but another type of evil increased that was not so obvious. It was the cultural acceptance of what is evil and immoral. People had become more comfortable with things not pleasing to God. People had relaxed into that false comfort and even celebrated it, because culture had accepted it. Things that were once considered evil and immoral had become acceptable and even commonplace. Then, in the dream, a friend of mine came to me and said, "It is becoming more difficult to fish." My friend meant fishing for people in the Biblical sense, as when Jesus told Peter and Andrew he would make them fishers of men, in spreading the gospel, the good news of Jesus Christ. It had become more difficult to "fish," because of rules and regulations created by our secular society. Soon thereafter, in my dream, we were fined for "fishing," as it had become a misdemeanor. Then, after a time, "fishing" became a felony, punishable by prison and/or death, because society had deemed it so.

I was praying about controlling my tongue. Later that night, in a dream, I heard the Lord say, "How do you love others when they are not around?" As Christians, as believers in Jesus Christ, we are to be known by our love. We can do this face to face, and we can also love others by controlling our tongue when we are not face to face. It's the things we say when others are not present.

I had a dream of a bride. I dreamt I was laying things on the ground in front of her, in her way, so she would trip or so she could not continue. I dreamt I was doing other things to throw her off and block her way, which made it difficult for her to move forward with her marriage. When I awoke, I perceived obstacles we create for others that keep them from coming to Christ or moving forward in their relationship with Christ.

I had a dream of heaven, and I was looking down on a very large mass of people. There was a narrow road running through the middle of the people. The masses of people lined both sides of the narrow road. Then, as I watched from above, I saw a person running down the middle of the road; and the people who lined the sides of the road were cheering them on and welcoming them. They shouted praises, joyful praises, every time someone came running down the road.

I had a dream of our Father in heaven. In the dream, He was sad, saddened by people forgetting Him or not thanking Him. The dream was about how He enters people's lives and does many great things, both large and small, yet people neither recognize Him, nor thank Him, nor seek Him. It was a sad dream and helped me understand how God truly cares for others. Acknowledging Him and our gratitude to Him is important, even in the small things. We need to be grateful for the rising of the sun each day, and even for the breath in our lungs.

I had a dream I was in the passenger seat of a car, and Jesus was driving the car. In the dream, there was some kind of emergency, and we had to go to a hospital. I could see the hospital in the distance. It was about two or three traffic lights ahead. However, when we got to the first traffic light, Jesus made a left turn instead of going straight to the hospital. I started yelling at Jesus that he made a wrong turn. I kept yelling at him that He was going the wrong way and should turn around, but He kept driving down this other road. The whole time He was just sitting there, driving and smiling, full of peace, and was unmoved by me yelling at Him. When I became tired of yelling at Jesus, and saw I was getting nowhere with my demands, I began to look out the window at where we were going. We were traveling down a beautiful, countryside road. It was peaceful, and I began to relax and enjoy the ride. As we rode along, I began to see all of these churches that were in various degrees of disrepair.

Once thriving and beautiful spiritual houses, they were now in shambles. As I looked at the abandoned churches, I felt sorrowful, yet I could see beauty and potential in each church we passed. After a moment, I asked Jesus, "How long is this going to take?" He answered, "As long as it takes to fix your heart."

I had a dream with many jail cells filled with people. I heard the Lord Jesus say, "It is like you are killing Me when you don't share Me." There is life in Jesus. He lives in us through His Holy Spirit. I had an urgency to share Him. In the dream I also saw the verse from Isaiah 61:1 about proclaiming the Good News of salvation through Jesus Christ to set the captives free, as well as the verse in Luke 4:18 about Jesus speaking of Himself and the Good News. By not sharing the gospel, the Good News of Jesus Christ, people remain in prison and die in sin. When we share Jesus, we offer freedom and life eternal, as well as a new life here on earth, renewed with, and empowered by, the Holy Spirit, being sent to us by Jesus Christ when we believe in and accept him as our Savior. He lives through you and through others. It is important to keep the Spirit alive, like a great flame, for the next generation. In that dream I also heard God say how He hates when we misuse scripture. He hates when we bend or manipulate it into what we want, to further our cause, such as when we use it to guilt people, or when we use it out of context. It is meant for freedom, life, and love. Yes, it is used to teach, correct, and direct; but it is not meant to damn, isolate, judge, or condemn. Scripture is meant to draw people close to Jesus and bring them from death to life.

I had a dream in which I saw scripture, not any particular scripture, but just scripture. I then heard Jesus say, "I know they are hungry." In the dream, I then saw how people are both physically and spiritually hungry, and I had a keen awareness of this hunger. In my dream, I then realized Jesus was making me aware of when He was on earth, and how He was so aware of physical and spiritual hunger. Jesus did all He could while

He was here on earth. Now we are to do all we can for Him and for others.

I had a dream that greatly upset me about the church. In the dream, I was going to an old church, with exterior and interior walls made of large, gray stones. Oddly, my purpose for going to church was to be entertained or to see a concert, not to worship God. When I entered the church, there were people in the pews, not a large number, but enough to fill the church. In the front of the church, behind the pulpit, there was a large curtain. As I was looking around at the church and the people within it, the curtains at the front of the church parted, and behind the curtain was a huge and terrifying beast! It was frightening to see. The bottom of the beast was cone shaped and made of crushed bones. Its torso was like that of a human, but it was otherworldly, mutilated, and looked like exposed muscle and sinew. Its head was like a skull, and it wore a gold helmet made for war, for doing battle. The beast was screaming its battle plan and how it would destroy. Frightened and terrified, I ran from the church. When I found my way outside, I heard the people in the church begin to worship this beast. They sounded like a large choir, like a great number of the people. Very disturbing.

I had a dream in which I heard Jesus ask, "What are you doing?" It made me think of the parable in Matthew 24 where the master of the house left a servant in charge of all the other servants, to give them food when they needed, and the master went away for a long time, but returned home unexpectedly.

I had a dream in which I heard a great number of voices crying out, "Save me!" It was the lost souls, and the sound was both pitiful and disturbing.

I had a dream I was yelling at a cocoon to open and become a beautiful butterfly. I was impatient and screaming at the cocoon. Then, I realized God's perfect timing and how silly I am to want things to hurry. For beauty comes in perfect timing, and no sooner. Sooner is to gratify myself and not honor God and His plan.

I had a vision about the first moment when Christ's blood hit the earth and was sprayed on people. Jesus shed His blood for the forgiveness of sins. My vision continued with the Roman guards flogging Jesus. They were sinning against Jesus, the Son of God, yet His blood was sprinkling and spattering them, giving them the opportunity for forgiveness, at the same time, if they believed He was the Son of God. Then I heard Him say, "And so I have forgiven you."

I had been praying to the Lord about self-hatred and about my fear of people. God gave me a vision of myself being angry at a flower and hating it. In the vision, I was looking at this beautiful flower and hating it with intensity. The Lord showed me He created the flower, and He created me. He showed me that hating the flower was like hating myself.

I heard the Lord say, "You want the trouble to go." Then the Lord impressed upon me the first step in ridding the trouble is toward Him. Trouble will not go away when we only use our own power, but only by the power of God will it go.

I had a dream where I was out into very deep space, and the earth was but a mere speck. As I was looking at the earth, I heard a heartbeat. Then, with each beat of the heart, the earth came more into view. I saw the earth closer and closer. It was God's heartbeat and love for us all.

# CHAPTER 10

# WORDS OF LOVE AND ENCOURAGEMENT

Now to each one the manifestation of the Spirit is given for
the common good.
To one there is given through the Spirit
a message of wisdom,
to another a message of knowledge
by means of the same Spirit,
to another faith by the same Spirit,
to another gifts of healing by that one Spirit,
to another miraculous powers,
to another prophecy,
to another distinguishing between spirits,
to another speaking in different kinds of tongues,
and to still another the interpretation of tongues.
All these are the work of one and the same Spirit,
and He distributes them to each one,
just as He determines.

1 Corinthians 12:7-11

But the one who prophesies speaks to people for their
strengthening, encouraging, and comfort.

1 Corinthians 14:3

In this chapter, I want to share with you some of the words of
love and encouragement I have heard from the Lord over the
years to share with others. I pray these words and messages
encourage and strengthen you.

Though a vandal may come and try to destroy a temple, My Spirit still dwells within its walls. It doesn't make the temple less
holy. You are holy. Though they crucified My Son's body, beaten
and torn and bloodied, was He any less holy? You are holy, and
what I call holy is holy. Receive it.

Tend My garden (perceiving we are to care for Christ's people). Each person is like a flower. They are all unique; each an individual and needing special care.

In the dark of the night, I have heard your every call for help, your every sorrow, your every praise. I have listened. I have heard. Your heart's cry has come to My ear. My Spirit has hovered over you. Do you think if you chose Me I would turn a deaf ear to those who belong to Me? No, precious child. I know the depths of your heart. I wade there, listening, loving, knowing. Through the shallows and through the deep, I have waded into all waters with you. My staff has protected you in the unseen from many things of which you are unaware. For I love you. I am closer than you think. I am within and without you. I hear you. (Perceive the personification of God; and if He were right there in front of you with all His promises and His character, just because you do not see Him, it does not mean He is untrue to whom He is.) I am the Way. All things come through Me. Lean on Me. Listen to My heart, for you and for all people. So much awaits you.

There was a time when you were "sorry" before Me. (Perceive being penitent, sorry for the things you have done.) Move on from there. (Perceive staying in a place of being sorry, but not receiving God's grace and mercy and moving forward. No one is keeping you in that place. It is hindering you from hearing and seeing all that God has for you.) I can only die so many times! (Perceive this was said lightly and humorously. Once and for all Jesus died for you. Do not hold Him on the cross in your life or stay in a place of suffering. Move forward, and walk out of the grave into life and His resurrection power.) You are a temple of the Holy Spirit! Lift your head!

My love hangs in the sky over you, waiting to be received. Do you not know? I have surrounded you with angels. I have been covering you and protecting you. You ask, "Why?" I say, "You are worth it!" (This was said emphatically, after which I felt a DEEP longing from God toward you. It is a desire for you and a deep love, a longing and waiting love.)

Like the rays of the sun, My love surrounds you. Just because you do not see it does not mean it does not exist.

My wing span is larger than you think. I have been coming to you your whole life, but you do not see Me. (I am praying your eyes open to see Jesus in people, places, and His creation. I am asking God to show Himself to you in a way you can understand and that it stays with you.) My wings are like the rays of the sun.

Many seedlings will grow from your wake. My Spirit will flow through you like water, watering the seeds I lay before you. You will water the seeds as you pass by. The birds of the air will rest in the trees when they mature one day. What is planted in love will surely grow and bloom. The wake of My love is the wake of your love. Where will the birds rest if you do not love, if you do not plant, if you do not water? Who will provide shade for the future? Walk and move in confidence. I have clothed you in righteousness and love. Walk and praise. Walk and plant. Move.

And the Spirit of God hovered in the air over you and led you.

I am here to love you, not dominate you.

My Spirit is like a mountain. Who can move it? It is moved by a compassionate heart. It is moved by faith. It is moved by love. It is moved by mercy.

I heard God speak the word "Unveiling." I perceived that is how the Lord looks at you. It is like a groom when he lifts the veil of his beloved bride. He lifts the veil and gazes upon her with such deep love, tenderness, and excitement, as well as a tremendous amount of emotion; so the Lord looks on you.

God showed me one day that His love and His words of love over our lives are like waves that hit the shore, constant and continual. Sometimes, His love and words of love are a gentle lapping. Other times, God's love and words of love grow loud and powerful, like waves that pound the seashore.

My Holy Spirit was released on the cross. Who can undo that? Who can cause it to go back? It was released. It will be accomplished. It is life. It cannot be removed.

I was standing in my kitchen one day, looking out the window, and I was thinking about something my husband does that challenges me and frustrates me. I said, "God, how am I going to deal with that the rest of our marriage?" I heard Him respond, "My work isn't good enough for you?" The Lord is always growing, changing, and transforming us if we allow Him. Have grace. God is working in you, as well as in others around you.

The sun will not set on My love for you.

I am life itself. Look around you. I am in all. Breath and life are Mine. I hold them in My hand. All has come through Me and belongs to Me. Your breath is Me (meaning Jesus wants you to know how expansive He is). All things come through Me. I did not just hang on a tree, I am the tree. I am life itself. My Spirit went out (perceive the Holy Spirit leaving Christ's body on the cross for all to receive). Will I not climb every mountain with you? Will I not weather all storms with you? (He asks as He shows His great devotion to you.)

I am the God of the universe. I am big and wide and unfathomable, and I cover and protect you. I care for you and place my garment over you.

Treat her well (as Jesus was speaking of His church, and I then felt His deep love for her.)

My Spirit has guided you in all things. (I perceived for this person that if God is not moving at the time, it's okay to rest. He will begin guiding again after rest has taken place. It does not mean He will not ever move again. It means rest is needed. It's not "over." God does not leave willing hearts waiting.)

I am not just a song. I am the song, the Song of Life, the Word itself; and it is a beautiful melody.

Know My great love for you. It is so deep and caring. I see you, I come to you, and I comfort you; all because you are Mine. I am devoted to you and your well-being. I see you. You are known by Me, the King of kings and Lord of lords. So deep and wide is My never-ending love for you. Move in and out of My love for you, like a breath. Breathe Me in. Receive My love. Breathe Me out. Give My love. Your story is My story. I long for you.

I carried love on my back for you (perceive Jesus carrying the cross for you), because I love you so. Each step was in love for you to know Me. Now, I carry you in love. I have carried you throughout your life and will continue to carry you all of your days, until I carry you into eternity.

I placed Myself as an offering for you. (Perceive Jesus before God, asking to be an offering, like someone throwing themselves over the top of another person for protection to save them.) Because I love you so, My heart was upraised for you (in a position of sacrifice, facing up). I sacrificed My love, place, and position for you. (Jesus came to earth to be a sacrifice for you.)

Don't fall back on what you know. Fall on Me, and I will lift you.

Open your eyes. What do you see? Close your eyes. What do you see? Whether there is light or darkness, I am there loving you. Whether you see Me in a moment or you do not, I am there loving you. I loved you before time began, and I will love you into eternity. My love does not fade or leave. It is like a flame that cannot be extinguished.

Though people may be far away from Me or near to Me, I will teach you wisdom. I will teach you love for My Name's sake. Come, walk with Me. There is no one I do not call. There is not one for whom I did not die. I desire all. I desire all to be reconciled to Me. I desire all to be with Me in eternity. I call to all. Listen, My voice rings throughout time for all. Matchless wonder. Matchless grace. Did I die to save only a few? I died for all.

Do not self-condemn, for I have called you, and I call you chosen and clean.

You have followed me for many years. Will I not lead you now? Hold out your hands, and I will take hold of them. Hold out your hands and I will release your worries.

Many people look at their age and consider what they have not done. Look at what I have done. (The Lord wants us to reflect on what He has done for us over the years and how powerful He has been in our lives and the lives of others.)

You are a mirror image of Me. (When you look in the mirror, you are a mirror image of God and His Glory. It sorrows Him when you look upon yourself negatively, no matter your age.)

I am the Light shining in the darkness, and I came for you in power. Who will stay My hand or keep Me from the ones I love and call My own? NO ONE. I am firm. (What God says is final. No one gets in His way or detours Him. He is solid.) I am the One who makes things grow. When I say, "Grow," they grow. When I say, "Bloom," they bloom. Who can stop Me and My desires? I desire you and call you. I caused you to grow. I caused you to bloom. Know Me. While things grow and bloom, they sing of My Glory. The birds of the air flock to Me when I call. What I say happens, whether in your time or Mine. What I say comes to pass. (Perceive God wants you to be confident in His power, regardless of whether you see the results in your lifetime. Be confident in His ability to accomplish what He says He will do.)

The door through which you passed was opened by Me. It cannot be shut. (God wants us to know our purpose. Only your own inactivity and failure to follow the Lord and do what He says will hinder your purpose. When a door is opened, walk through it. It is your choice when you enter through the doorway to keep going or to simply stand in the doorway and not move.)

See the forest through the trees. (Perceive this is a deep, deep forest, a heavenly deep forest.) On high, in the heavens, there

I am, aware of you. To you there is a forest, but I see you. (This is Jesus aware of you. You may not think He sees or knows you, or you may think you are just one of many, but that is not true. He does see you. He sees you as an individual, not just one of many. He sees you deeply and intimately. You are unique; created and loved that way by God. He loves you in the unique way you need to be loved.)

I was not going to let you walk the path alone. There is an open road before you, and I am with you. It is a path of beauty and love, accompanied by Me. In things you do not see beauty, I call forth beauty. (Perceive how God pulls forth beauty from things we may not consider to be beautiful.) Consider a tree that has fallen in the woods. It rots and decays, but I cause things to grow and bloom from it. It feeds other things. Consider My death on the cross and the life that has come forth saving many. There is beauty. It is about how you see things. The sun rises and sets on My command. Can I not make what I see beautiful? Can I not do all things? My mouth opens, and universes are born. I create out of nothing. Will I not make it beautiful? A choir of angels sing before Me. Will I not sing over you? I delight in you, precious one. I delight in you. Do not be afraid. Let go. Walk. Come. Your path is beautiful, because I speak into it. You are clothed in My Spirit, given for you. I wait for you and call you to a life of freedom. (Perceive Jesus is saying, "Come on!" It is like diving off a diving board into the deep end, and your father is urging you to jump so he can catch you. You will be okay.)

There is no thing I cannot do. From dawn until dusk, from day to evening, I am the Lord; and the days and the evenings are Mine. I call the stars to come out and shine, and they do. Will I not help you? I give you light by day and by night. I have placed you. I hear your requests. Think on who I am and whose you are. I sent My Spirit to this earth to help you and embody you. You are not alone. I am with you. My love is vast. (God really wants you to know how big and vast He is and, likewise, so too His love. I also hear the word "magnitude." Meditate on it.) I shed My blood for you. Claim it over your situation.

The sun will not set on My love for you, but it will always burn bright. My love never fades or dies, but always burns bright. Rest in this. My love for you is real and deep. You cannot know or see its depths or heights. (It is like looking out into space or the ocean's depths.) Know it. It NEVER stops loving you.

Was My Spirit released to not be used? To not forgive? To not free the captives? No. LOVE. My love rises above it all. I am the God of love.

I created a piece of art for a woman who had a ministry that helped women who have been sex trafficked. While creating the piece, I heard the Lord say, "I draw them close to Me (God draws them close to Himself through you and your ministry). I created them for My Glory and will build them into good and pleasing spiritual houses. For My Name's sake, I will restore them, and they shall be renewed. I will redeem the springtime of their lives that were stolen from them. For I am the Lord, and no one can stay My plans or divert My great hand. They will be redeemed by My very hand. Each woman is precious to Me. They are close to Me and not far away. They each are like a thread in the train of My robe, part of Me. I care for them and wear their burdens. They are woven into the fabric of My being. Each woman will become a mighty oak. They will sit in the shade of My Tree of Life and be shielded by My very hand. They will be well watered by the words of your mouth I will give you for them from Me. I call them in love to come to Me. Teach them to be mighty women in Me. Share the love of Christ, and build them up in Me."

I created a piece of art for a woman who is a missionary to orphans in Africa and other parts of the world. As a message for that woman, I heard the Lord say, "You come bearing My mark and My seal. Nothing will come against you. You will know resistance, but they will be resisting Me. Know that you are safe and sealed and are cared for by My very hand. Nothing can come against My elect. Protected. Be on your knees for My activity in those around you. I will hear you and answer you, for your heart is good and filled with compassion for those around you. I do not desire for children to perish, for I am a God of life and love, not death and sorrow. I am the God of freedom, not captivity. I am on your side. My Spirit is given for you. My love for you is pure. Lean into Me, and I will lean into you. Grasp hold of Me, and I will place My cover over you. They will follow if you lead. I cause things to grow and bloom, even in the driest of places. All things grow and bloom when given and surrendered to Me. What seems hopeless will flourish. Your feet bring peace. I shine forth and go before you. Yes, a door is opened unto you so that children may call on My Name."

I created a piece of art for someone who had retired from the missionary field. As a message for the retired missionary, I heard the Lord say, "I have placed angels around you since your birth, for I have desired to draw you close to Me, because I love you and have plans for you. I hold you dear to Me. I led you to the water's edge and said, 'Drink. I will fill all your needs.' I led you to the water's edge and said, 'Trust Me. Have faith in Me. Seek Me, and I will show you wonders of mercy and grace for My people.' For I pour freely and call all to Me to drink and be filled with My love. Why do they resist? A tree grows in the garden. I planted a seed, watered it, and watched it grow. The seed I planted is in you. I am tender toward My creation. I am tender to each seed that is planted. You scattered seed for Me, and I have watered and pruned them by My hand. You have planted a forest for Me. You are engulfed in My Light. I surround you, because I love you. Oh, what will grow and bloom! (I keep hearing God say repeatedly, "Well done." This is like Jesus saying "Well done My good and faithful servant" in Matthew 25:21.) You have honored Me before men. I will honor you. I give you My love and My Light. I have loved you and guided you your whole life. So much abundance will be poured on you. Receive it with joy. My hand has been upon you and will be on you."

When you walk through the world, you see and experience many trials and suffering. But I am the Lord your provider; and I provide for all that you will need, beginning with My Spirit, the most powerful force. Nothing can come against My Spirit or the gift of eternal life promised through, and given by, My Son, Jesus, when you choose Him. You are my elect and chosen one. (Perceive this as the basis for rejoicing or why we can rejoice, because we have been given His Spirit.) Do not let darkness enter your mind. Bring your whole heart as a pleasing offering to Me. Follow the path of peace. (I am reminded of the scripture in Philippians 4:8 that reads, "whatever is true, whatever is noble, whatever is right, whatever is pure, whatever is lovely, whatever is admirable—if anything is excellent or praiseworthy—think about such things" when we have difficulty with people or a particular situation. Think specifically what is true, lovely, etc., about the person or the situation. It will help us "see" through God's eyes.)

I am here! (I heard this very loudly. It is is Jesus.) I am not encapsulated somewhere apart from you. I am within you!

I made you for love. Do not be dismayed, for I am He, the author of your life. Do you think I do not have a plan for you? Do I create without purpose? Seek Me, and you will find life to the fullest. I have good for you, child. Seek Me, for wisdom and understanding. Stand on My ground, and I will place you. Orient yourself by My Word and My direction. (I am given a vision of you standing in a great open area with nothing around you. All I see is land. There is dirt, but nothing growing in it. There is no grass. There are no trees. You seem a little panicky, looking around to find which way you should go. However, you are to stand where you are and cry out to the Lord for direction, asking Him what you are to do; and He will cause things to grow around you. I perceive you are to begin planting.)

What are you doing with what is around you? What are you doing with what has been given to you? (I perceive you have a blank canvas with much talent.) It is like a wide open field. Together we make beauty. Seek Me. My seed (Word) is life. Oh, what we can do! (I perceive you and God working together when you seek Him and what He wants for you. It is okay to trust Him with your life. Do not fear. We must have faith.) Open your hand. Allow Me to give you the life I have for you. You must open your hand and receive it. I freely give it to you. Your mountain seems jagged, but I make things smooth. Who am I? Who do you say I am when you encounter Me? You are not lost, but found by Me, the King of heaven and earth who loves you. I purchased you with My Son's blood just to have you near. You have many questions. Come to Me. Ask. Seek. Search. Do I create beauty for no reason? Do I give life for no reason? Come to Me with all things. You will not be abandoned. You will not be turned away. I do not harm, but love. I embrace you. When you walk through the valley, I am with you and beside you, protecting you. You are not alone. I have given Myself for you. I am bound to you and will not let you go. Live in freedom. Live in Me. I have given you My Spirit to guide you. Seek Me. Ask. Search. My great arm is constantly raised to ward off evil from you (like the apple of His eye, quick to protect). Much goes on you do not see (that is, work in the unseen, on your behalf, by the Lord). Look back in love, and you will see Me all along.

You are never in darkness, because you live in My Light.

I am with you in the night. It is never really dark for you, because I always shine on you whether you are awake or at rest, because I love you. I sacrificed Myself for you, because I love you so deeply, child. Oh, I gave and have given My all for you. You are like the rising of the sun, glorious. I sing over you day and night. My words of love for you wash over you like the tides. You are My child, and I declare you are glorious. My heart leads straight to yours. Your prayers are offered up to heaven, and I hear them. They are a sweet fragrance to Me. I love to hear from you, for you are my most precious child. You are glorious to Me, and I love to hear your voice. I am connected to you, in your heart and by My Spirit.

I am working on the inner man so that I may be glorified. It is not what you do in a course or in a classroom, but it is what I do within you. Seek Me.

Come, rest in Me, and take shelter in Me. (Perceive this is like the birds of the air who gather in trees at night, they trust the Lord God to protect them at night, when there is darkness all around, and they are easy prey. He protects them and allows them to rest so they may have strength for the next day.)

I purchased you with My blood. I will never discard you.

My arms are like mountains. Who shall fear? For those who seek refuge in Me shall be covered by Me, by My promises. Those who walk in My ways will find refuge—life and flowing water in the desert place. I am Holy. Only I can lead you through a desert to a place of plenty. Those who go into the desert and seek Me know the value of My Spirit. My Spirit is most precious and valuable. My Spirit is all you will ever need.

And they drank and were renewed.

Like a veil, My Great Spirit washed over them. Like water, My Spirit washed them and filled them, and they were renewed and refreshed like spring. The desert behind them, and My Glory before them, they walked in the confidence of My Spirit, which is living water. Come, wash in the water. Come, be clean, and I will give you living water!

And those who have been through the desert have been guided by the Spirit of the Living God. The Spirit will lead them to

Living Water, Everlasting Life; and they will thirst no more.

You will bloom again. Fear not, for I cause the flowers to bloom. (Perceive this is for your protection. Flowers bloom when they are supposed to bloom, for their protection and the fullness of their purpose, and not before their time. They too are vulnerable.)

My arms are big enough to hold you and all of your worries. The battle over you is won. Will I not continue to fight and protect the very one I fought so hard to win, the one for whom I shed My blood? I love you, child. I will act on your behalf. Though your path may be jagged at times, I, the Lord, will make your path straight, for I called you from a far off place and made a way for you to come to Me. Will I not make your way smooth? I died for you. Will I not be your advocate in all you do? Though the path may be jagged at times, your obedience unto Me will clear the path if you make a way for Me. The veil was torn in two, from top to bottom, not the other way. For My hand is mighty. The veil was torn for ALL!

At the foot of the cross,
You will find Me there.
Bend your knee and bow,
At the foot of the cross.
For there you shall see,
All you came to see,
At the foot of the cross.
Come to Me.
What were you seeking?
What did you find?
You may look,
You may search,
But with all of your heart,
Come to Me,
And,
At the foot of the cross,

You will see.
There.
Look to and for Me.

I will light your way.  I barred the way [of Satan, the evil one].
I fought for you and laid claim to you, and you are Mine.  I shine
forth in your life.  Unto Me (meaning you belong to Christ).  Nothing can come against My blood offering.  My blood was offered
for you, precious child.  Come.  Surrender, that I may have My
way in your life. It is not the end, but the beginning.

I have a never - ending love for you.  My love reaches across the
universe to touch you.  Reach back to Me.  My love is bright and
beautiful, never dull!

And the Glory of the Lord shone
In the valleys and the streams.
His Glory shone before me,
And I,
I was in awe of my Savior and Lord.
For His Glory filled the very sky I was under,
Like a great hand cupped over me.
I looked and saw His Glory.
And the mountains parted
By the power of His hand.
And I, His child,
Was freed.

# CHAPTER 11

## WORDS AND WATERCOLORS

**In the morning, LORD, you hear my voice;**
**in the morning I lay my requests before you**
**and wait expectantly.**

Psalm 5:3

This chapter contains poems, prayers, spontaneous water colors, and personal thoughts, as well as entries from my journal during, and towards the end of, the dark night. It also contains additional dreams and words of love and encouragement I have received from the Lord.

. . . . . . . . . . . . . . . . . . . . . . . . . . . . . . . . . . . . . . . . . . . . . . . . . . . . .

**I was praying to the Lord to help me with my art.**

**Precede me Lord.**

Lord, let the darkness, fear, anxiety, and self-doubt not overcome me, but let me be strong in You. Let me hear You and have joy in following You!

And God said, "With water and blood, I will protect her. She is Mine. Do not fear the darkness. I have overcome the darkness. I slayed it for you precious one. Do not be afraid. You are Mine."

I had a bad dream about the house in which I grew up. I dreamt of the chaos, dirt, and disorganization. I dreamt of the lack of structure and focus and how it was all around me. In the dream, I felt my fear and was reminded of my fear of people.

He said to me, "My love surrounds you and protects you."

My Lord Jesus stomps my fears. He heals and saves.

I heard the Lord speaking to me today while I worked.

"I will change you.
Be deliberate.   I am deliberate.
Be purposeful.  I am purposeful.
Do not wait.  Take charge, love.
I change you.  Be purposeful.
You can have it.  Be focused.
Do not go back and forth like the wind.
I change you.  My Word.
I am talking to you precious child.
I send My Spirit to you."

I say, thank You, Lord.  Thank You for showing me this.  I see
where You are showing me that if I am deliberate, focused,
and purposeful, my fear and anxiety will be reduced.  I am so
afraid of the darkness, but You are Light.

I had a dream where a friend of mine was showing me a little terra cotta mosaic painting. I could see all the little pieces of the mosaic coming together to create the beautiful painting. Over the top of the mosaic was a blue bird.

A couple of weeks later, I was in a store and saw a magnet that had a blue bird on it. The magnet said, "It's never too late to have a happy childhood." I saw another magnet that said, "It's never too late to be who you might have been." Thank You Lord!

I am the Lord. I heal you.
I mend your hurt childhood.
I open old wounds to heal them.
I place My hands on them.
They are a sweet, soothing salve.
I am the Lord, who heals you.

The love in Jesus's blood heals.
His blood washes our wounds.

I surround you with
My Light
My love
My Spirit
My Son
I gave.

Lately, Lord, I am finally beginning to feel Your love. I have been praying for a love relationship with You for so long. I am no longer feeling anxious, condemned, horrible, and purposeless. I am feeling loved by You and that You have given me a purpose. I have never felt this way in my life. I did not know this feeling in life was possible. You are here, and You love me; and I know it, or rather, I am beginning to know it. Thank You for answering this prayer. I love You too!

How deep
And how wide,
My love is
For you.
Like the rolling sea,
My love washes.
Like the depths of the sea,
Like the expanse of space,
It is unknown.

I am the Light
In the darkness.
Hope.
I send My Spirit.
It goes before
You.
Look for Me,
Child.

I had a dream of this little girl who was about seven years old. She had blond straggly hair, and she had been abused. God the Father was holding her. The Father held the little girl, but then He handed her to me. I felt happy and joyful. I told the little girl in a very excited way, "Jesus loves you!" I was so happy to tell her, because she had been abused; and I tried to help her understand Jesus loves her, but she could not. She did not think anyone really loved her. I sang, "Jesus Loves Me" to her. She began to smile as I held her. She began to realize that, in fact, Jesus does love her. We smiled and sang together.

When I woke, I realized the little girl was me, or part of me. She is healed by the love of Jesus. Thank You Jesus!

"Sharing Jesus's love with the hurt child inside me"

My Spirit goes out,
Before you,
Child,
Like a dove,
Gentle and sweet,
Leaving the smallest
Breeze.

You are My bride.
No matter what,
You belong to Me,
Always.

Lord, I want to be reverent before You.
Please help me.
Please change my heart.

I have been trying to concentrate on a loving relationship with God and His purpose for me. It is helping me to calm my thoughts and feelings and to not be so anxious. A love relationship with God is wonderful. It is something I am constantly learning about, how He loves us so much and how He desires for us to love Him. I am learning to focus on God and to receive His love. How beautiful; and thank You, Lord. Please help my relationship with you grow.

Love for you,
Precious child.
Love.
Take My love,
Precious one.
I Am the One.
We are one,
One in Love.

## "The Lesson"

I am crying for you,
Child.
You are sad.
I show Myself to you,
Child.
Yet, you look
To the world,
And worldly things,
Child.
I am enough for you,
Child.
Are My Spirit
And My Son,
Not enough for you,
Child?
I comfort you,
Child.
My love for you is unending,
Child.
Child,
You are Mine.

I had a dream about my friend who is a pastor. I saw the Holy Spirit descend upon her and saw beautiful colors around her. Because the Holy Spirit was coming upon her, all of these beautiful colors and lights from the Lord emanated everywhere from her.

Holy one,
Holy one,
I cloak you.
Holy one,
Holy one,
I place a cover,
Over you.

I had a dream in which I was walking alone down a road. I walked and walked until, at some point, I saw my son. He smiled and wanted to be with me. I told him I was on a long, hard walk, and it was dangerous. He still wanted to be with me. I told him it was okay to come, but it would be a long, hard walk. He responded, "It is worth it to see the Son."

In the beginning,
God created.
In the beginning,
Is the beginning,
Of faith in Him.
He separates light,
From darkness,
In us.
This means taking in,
His Son.
Believing,
In the beginning,
Is the beginning.

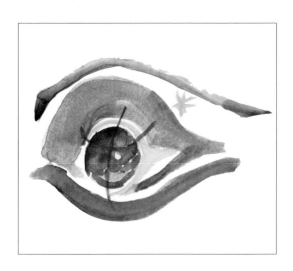

Come into My love.
My love casts a shadow
Of Light over you,
From generation,
To generation.

Oh Lord,
Your Glory is aflame before me.
In Your Light and in Your love is unending grace.
I lay myself before You.
Before You I am cleansed.
Before You my sins are forgiven.
Before You I am humble.
Before You I receive mercy.
Before You I am loved.

I had a vision of a rose floating on water inside a glass, which was shaped like a brandy snifter. The rose was a "peace" rose. It was protected by the glass and had some water to help it live. Fragile, yet protected by living water, it was an isolated, protected beauty.

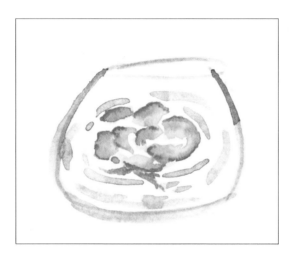

Lord, thank You for peace.
Thank You for protection.
Thank You for Living Water.
I am seeing Your love for me.
That is a prayer answered.

My love brings hope.
My love washes down,
On you,
Like a river
Running down a mountain,
To a valley,
Nourishing the fields below.
My love seeps.
My love saturates.
My love penetrates,
Your whole being.
Like water,
My love
Will wash over you,
Within and without.

I am in the shield of
My Father's love.
Evil cannot penetrate
My Father's love,
For me.
He shields and protects me,
With His love.
No harm will come near.
Lord, help me
To not sin against You.
Thank You,
For love, grace, and mercy.

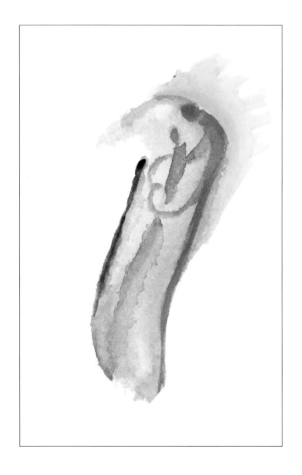

**Thank You, Lord, for rescuing me from darkness.**

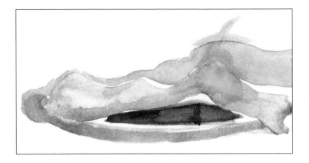

Even though you have been in the valley,
My love has surrounded you.
Even though you have been surrounded
With rough, jagged mountains to climb,
In love, I placed hope atop them.
Because of My love for you,
I surrounded you.
Though you did not see me,
I was there.

Lord, I feel angry and frustrated.
Help me to start believing what You say.

My love overcomes
Anger and frustration.
My love replaces anger.
My love is over anger.
Love is,
I Am,
Is love.

Lord, thank You for these verses.  They touch my heart.
Thank You for loving me and saving me.

Psalm 18: 16 – 19, 28

He reached down from on high and took hold of me;
he drew me out of deep waters.
He rescued me from my powerful enemy,
from my foes, who were too strong for me.
They confronted me in the day of my disaster,
but the Lord was my support.
He brought me out into a spacious place;
he rescued me because he delighted in me.
You, Lord, keep my lamp burning;
my God turns my darkness into light.

# I am free!
## I am saved!
### Today!

I had a dream about my childhood neighborhood, and I was playing "Ring Around the Rosie" in the grass. In the dream, I knew something bad happened here; but whatever happened, the Lord wanted to heal. When I woke, I thought about the game, "Ring Around the Rosie," and how, in ashes, in the game, we all fall down; but in life, we do not have to wear the ashes forever. We get back up with the Lord's help, healing, and cleansing. He does not want us to stay in, or be covered by, ashes.

I dance with Jesus.
I dance with my King.
In the safety of His arms,
I dance with my King.
We play "Ring Around the Rosie,"
Jesus and I.
We smile, hold hands,
And look at each other in the eye.
We smile and dance.
We dance in a ring,
Jesus and I.
"We all fall down."
He never lets go, my hand in His.
With the breath of His mouth,
He smiles and breathes,
Not wanting any ashes, to stick to me.
He draws me close and hugs me.
We smile and dance.
I love You, Jesus, my King.

On the plain
and in the valley,
where the water flows,
I am there.
Where the flowers are gold
And the river flows,
I am there.
There are giants
in the valley
And on the plain.
Yet, where there are giants,
Inside thee is the greatest.
For I dwell in thee.
You see, in the valley,
A river flows.
Bend your knee and drink,
For the River of Life flows
From Me.
You are sustained in Me, child.

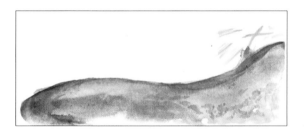

From the tip of the mountain,
to the base of the mountain,
Your love washes over me like gold.
From its purple peaks,
To its lush green fields,
Your love rushes over me.
It rushes down over me,
Wearing away my iniquities.
All my transgressions
Become as silt.
I become soft, pliable clay,
For You, Mighty One,
To mold, each day.

Life in Me. Life in Me.
The River of Life is in Me.
I pour life and Living Water into thee.
Count on Me.
Live in Me.
Love in Me.
Be in Me.
I will not fail you. Trust in Me.
I do not break promises.
I am not a man, like thee.
The River of Life flows from Me.
Do not despair. Trust in Me.
Be in Me.
Do not be afraid. My Spirit is in thee.
Go forth, our hands entwined,
Fingers clasped, and wound up in Mine.
Have confidence in Me and the River of Life
That flows from Me.

Gather for Me child. Bring them all to Me.
Do not be afraid. Bring them all to Me.
My love is deeper than the sea.
Find strength in Me.
Be in Me,
Then you will be, strong as a mighty wave,
Fluid and flowing, for all to see.
Like a wave, you will rise and crest,
And when you peak, you will see,
The great numbers, you bring to Me.
See them all, like fish in the sea,
Shimmering and shining,
Moving in Me.
Yes, a mighty wave,
With a school of fish,
Visible to Me,
Shining and shimmering,
Waiting for Me.
Yes, gather for Me child.

Remember Me.
I am the Living Water.
I am the flowers in the field.
I am the grassy plain.
I am wide.
I am tall.
I am in the quiet.
I am in the soft spot,
To lay your head.
I am love.
I am Light.
There is no thing
I cannot do.
Come, take your place,
In Me.
My arms are open.
My table is ready.
Come, bring your gifts.
Do not look around,
but look at Me.
Take the steps, child.
Be confident in Me.
Remember Me
And Who I am.
I am, I Am.

My arms are open for you.
Come.
I died for you.
Be in Me.
Be confident in Me.
You are safe in Me.
I am in you.
You have the Holy Spirit.
Trust Me.
Speak the truth in Me.
Obey Me and My commands.
Love.
Speak in love and truth.
Place your feet on the ground,
And walk.

How great is Your love, Oh God.
It fills the earth and sky.
I hear and feel Your love,
In the wind on the grassy plain.
It ripples and waves.
I bend and bow.
I hear and feel Your love,
In the echo of a sound,
From the peak of a mountain.
Yes, Your love rings over and over.
Though we throw stones,
You are merciful in Your unfailing love.
Your love falls on me,
Like rain from the sky.
I am drenched with it.
Your love swells around me,
Like an approaching wave.
I am lifted up,
And my feet flutter,
Off the sandy bottom.
I float on Your love and lie back.
You do not let me sink.
Your love and Light shine on me,
Oh Lord.

You absorb all
My pain and sorrows,
Oh Lord.
You lift my burdens
From me,
Oh Lord.
Yet, Your grace falls
On me,
Oh Lord.
I lean into You,
Oh Lord.
I desire to sink
Into You,
Oh Lord.
Oh, to be a drop of water
That falls into the sea
Of Your vast love,
And become part of You,
Flowing and moving in You,
Oh Lord,
with fluid freedom.

Now child, your garden will grow.
It will grow in love for Me.
I will plant seeds in you.
You will be a beautiful rose garden for Me.
Covered in roses,
My bride to be.
Leave your past,
And come to Me.
I will plant a garden in thee.
Watch it grow.
Watch it bloom.
Patience.
I will care for you.
I will tend you.
I will water you.
I will not let you wither or die.
I will protect you from scorching sun.
Flood waters will not overcome you.
I will not let words overtake you.
I will not let you lie bare.
I will cover you.
I will protect you.
For you are Mine,
To tend and care.

The glassy sea
The glassy sea
My Son rises over the glassy sea.
He rises in Glory.
Storms and tumultuous waves
Are swept back.
The weight of His love
Moves all.
His love slowly presses downward,
Creating,
A smooth glassy sea.

**Living Water flows from My Son.**

Unforgiveness child,
Can turn the reddest of roses
Into a dark, blackening storm.
My Son died for forgiveness,
A gift freely given.
Unforgiveness causes the blackest of sins.
The darkest storms will swirl about,
Created by the complications of the mind.
The simplicity of forgiveness is forgotten,
When the mind rages and storms over injustice.
Darkness looms and sin crouches,
While My Son patiently waits
To offer you His peace.
Do not harden your heart with unforgiveness.
Call My Son to the center of your storm.
Calm and peace await you,
While your thoughts thunder about.
Invite My Son into the center.
Feel His love and calm.
Let My Son become the eye in your storm,
From which you see the gift of peace He has for you.
See your storm through His eyes.
Watch as the rains fall.
Watch as the storm dissipates.
Watch the winds change.
Watch as the storm drifts over the horizon.
Watch it fade into the distance.
My Son will remove it from your life
And from your sight.
Blessed is he who walks in His ways,
Calming the storms of unforgiveness,
Asking for healing from the raging storm.
My Son, the Prince of Peace,
Almighty is He.
He makes your way smooth
Upon land and sea.
Ask Him to enter
The blackest of storms,

The blackest of sins,
The darkest of hours,
The deepest, darkest, unforgiveness,
Bringing His Light,
Bringing His love,
Bringing His peace.
Watch His blood turn the blackest storm
Into the reddest rose.
My Son, the Prince of Peace,
Died for forgiveness.
Listen to Him.

I had a dream there was a great, vast plain or valley; and I saw the earth open and create a hole like a big well. It was deep. I looked into the well and saw water rising. Yet, each time I thought I saw the bottom, or the source of the well, I would find another opening and even more water. It went so very deep! It was like a well within a well within a well. Is this like Living Water, Lord? It never runs out. It is so very deep we cannot see or understand its depths or source? Thank You for this, Lord.

Child,
Living Water pours forth from Me,
Like a great waterfall.
It crashes down, yet spreads into a pool.
Bend and drink.
My arms are like streams,
Flowing from the mountaintop,
Embracing and giving life to all.
My shoulders are like mountains,
Mighty and tall,
Large enough to carry the greatest of burdens.
Come, find peace and life, in Me.
I provide all you need,
Child.

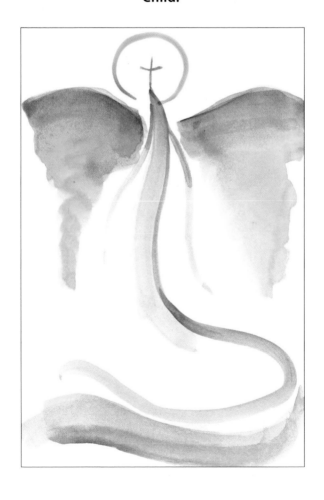

Child,
I am the maker of heaven and earth.
I rule over all.
I will show you the way.
I will place your steps.
Trust in Me, child.
Child of God,
Child of God,
I, the Lord, love you,
Child of God.
My mercy reigns.
All in heaven know My Name.
I
Am a child,
Of the King.
He loves me.
He knows me.
He calls me by name.
I
Am a child,
Of the King,
Set on earth
To praise His Name,
Set on earth
To give glory to Him,
Who called me
By name.
I
Am a child,
Of the King.
I
Am a child,
Of the King.
He loves me.
He knows me.
He calls me by name.

I
Am a child,
Of the King,
Set on earth
To praise His Name,
Set on earth
To give glory to Him,
Who called me
By name.
I
Am a child,
Of the King.

Oh Lord,
I turn my face to You.
You clothe me in righteousness.
You surround me with Your Glory.
You wash me and make me clean.
You shower me with love and mercy.
Grace is Your way.
Your love is everlasting.
Your will and way are perfect.
Let me follow You, Lord, all of my days.
Let me shine for You.
Let me hide no more, but boldly proclaim
Your Name,
Your mercy,
Your love,
Your grace,
Your Word,
The truth.
Let me praise You, Lord.
Let Your Glory shine,
Oh Lord.

Then I heard a loud voice in heaven say: "Now have come the salvation and the power and the kingdom of our God, and the authority of his Messiah. For the accuser of our brothers and sisters, who accuses them before our God day and night, has been hurled down. **They triumphed over him by the blood of the Lamb and by the word of their testimony."**
Revelation 12:10,11

Now, I encourage you to go and tell what the Lord Jesus has done for you.

**If you do not yet know God or His love, you can welcome Him into your heart by believing and praying this prayer:**

Lord God, Creator of All,
You know me and love me. You sent Your only Son, Jesus, to die for me for the forgiveness of all my sins, so we may be one and so I may have eternal life. I choose to accept Your Son, Jesus, into my heart and believe in Him. Forgive me of my sins, Lord. Through Jesus, You have cleansed me and made me whole. I am a new creation, forgiven and free. Bring me into a new life with You and into a new purpose in You. May I glorify You in all that I do. I receive You. I receive Your Son, Jesus. I receive the Holy Spirit. Thank You, Lord.
I pray in the name of Christ Jesus.

Amen.

In that day you will say:
"I will praise you, Lord.
Although you were angry with me,
your anger has turned away
and you have comforted me.
Surely God is my salvation;
I will trust and not be afraid.
The Lord, the Lord himself, is my strength and my defense;
he has become my salvation."
With joy you will draw water
from the wells of salvation.
In that day you will say:
"Give praise to the Lord, proclaim his name;
make known among the nations what he has done,
and proclaim that his name is exalted.
Sing to the Lord, for he has done glorious things;
let this be known to all the world.
Shout aloud and sing for joy, people of Zion,
for great is the Holy One of Israel among you."

Isaiah 12:1-6


... you may have had to suffer grief in all kinds of trials.
These have come so that the proven genuineness of your
faith – of greater worth than gold,
which perishes even though refined by fire –
may result in praise, glory,
and honor when Jesus Christ is revealed.

1 Peter 1: 6,7

# AFTERWORD

God has done a great work in me, and I will not be ashamed.
God has done great things for me, and I acknowledge Him
and praise Him.
God has recreated me and made me new, and I thank Him.
God has brought forth beauty from the ashes of my life.

I want to thank my precious husband for always being at my
side, encouraging me and helping me with whatever I ask.
I want to thank my children for giving me grace and for encouraging me to tell this story of God's transformative power and
His ability to heal and to save. I want to thank my friends who
prayed for me and encouraged me while writing this book.
I want to thank my friend, Jeanne Sperry, for her generous and
patient spirit in helping me layout this book. I want to thank
God for all He has done and will do, for me, and for you.

# END NOTES

Dr. Brian Simmons, The Psalms: Poetry on Fire,
The Passion Translation®
Translated directly from the original Hebrew text
(Racine Wisconsin: BroadStreet Publishing Group, LLC, 2015), 61.